REGENTS RENAISSANCE DRAMA SERIES

General Editor: Cyrus Hoy
Advisory Editor: G. E. Bentley

A FAIR QUARREL

THOMAS MIDDLETON
and
WILLIAM ROWLEY

A Fair Quarrel

Edited by

GEORGE R. PRICE

UNIVERSITY OF NEBRASKA PRESS · LINCOLN

Library of Congress Cataloging in Publication Data

Middleton, Thomas, d. 1627.
    A fair quarrel.

    (Regents Renaissance drama series)
    Published in 1617 under title: A faire quarrell.
    Includes bibliographical references.
    I. Rowley, William, 1585?–1642?, joint author.
II. Title.
PR2714.F3   1976   822′.3   74–33674
ISBN 0–8032–0299–7

Regents Renaissance Drama Series

The purpose of the Regents Renaissance Drama Series is to provide soundly edited texts, in modern spelling, of the more significant plays of the Elizabethan, Jacobean, and Caroline theater. Each text in the series is based on a fresh collation of all sixteenth- and seventeenth-century editions. The textual notes, which appear above the line at the bottom of each page, record all substantive departures from the edition used as the copy-text. Variant substantive readings among sixteenth- and seventeenth-century editions are listed there as well. In cases where two or more of the old editions present widely divergent readings, a list of substantive variants in editions through the seventeenth century is given in an appendix. Editions after 1700 are referred to in the textual notes only when an emendation originating in some one of them is received into the text. Variants of accidentals (spelling, punctuation, capitalization) are not recorded in the notes. Contracted forms of characters' names are silently expanded in speech prefixes and stage directions, and, in the case of speech prefixes, are regularized. Additions to the stage directions of the copy-text are enclosed in brackets. Stage directions such as "within" or "aside" are enclosed in parentheses when they occur in the copy-text.

Spelling has been modernized along consciously conservative lines. "Murther" has become "murder," and "burthen," "burden," but within the limits of a modernized text, and with the following exceptions, the linguistic quality of the original has been carefully preserved. The variety of contracted forms (*'em, 'am, 'm, 'um, 'hem*) used in the drama of the period for the pronoun *them* are here regularly given as *'em*, and the alternation between *a'th'* and *o'th'* (for *on* or *of the*) is regularly reproduced as *o'th'*. The copy-text distinction between preterite endings in *-d* and *-ed* is preserved except where the elision of *e* occurs in the penultimate syllable; in such cases, the final syllable is contracted. Thus, where the old editions read "threat'ned," those of the present series read "threaten'd." Where, in the old editions, a contracted preterite in -*y'd* would yield -*i'd* in modern spelling (as in "try'd," "cry'd," "deny'd"), the word is here given in its full form (e.g., "tried," "cried," "denied").

Punctuation has been brought into accord with modern practices. The effort here has been to achieve a balance between the generally light pointing of the old editions, and a system of punctuation which, without overloading the text with exclamation marks, semicolons, and dashes, will make the often loosely flowing verse (and prose) of the original syntactically intelligible to the modern reader. Dashes are regularly used only to indicate interrupted speeches, or shifts of address within a single speech.

Explanatory notes, chiefly concerned with glossing obsolete words and phrases, are printed below the textual notes at the bottom of each page. References to stage directions in the notes follow the admirable system of the Revels editions, whereby stage directions are keyed, decimally, to the line of the text before or after which they occur. Thus, a note on 0.2 has reference to the second line of the stage direction at the beginning of the scene in question. A note on 115.1 has reference to the first line of the stage direction following line 115 of the text of the relevant scene.

CYRUS HOY

The University of Rochester

Contents

List of Abbreviations

Brooks   Jerome E. Brooks. *Tobacco: Its History Illustrated by the Books, Manuscripts, and Engravings in the Library of George Arents, Jr. . . . 4* vols. New York, 1938.

Bullen   A. H. Bullen, ed. *The Works of Thomas Middleton,* vol. 4. 8 vols. Boston, 1885–86.

corr.   corrected

Dyce   Alexander Dyce, ed. *The Works of Thomas Middleton,* vol. 3. 5 vols. London, 1840.

Gale   Thomas Gale. *Certaine Workes of Chirurgerie.* London, 1586.

Gibson   Edmund Gibson. *Codex Juris Ecclesiastici Anglicani: or, The Statutes, Constitutions, Canons, Rubricks, and Articles of the Church of England . . . .* 2 vols. Oxford, 1761.

OED   *Oxford English Dictionary*

Oliphant   E. H. C. Oliphant, ed. *Shakespeare and His Fellow Dramatists,* vol. 2. 2 vols. New York, 1929.

Q1   The First Quarto, 1617

Q2   The Second Quarto, 1622

Sampson   Martin W. Sampson, ed. *Thomas Middleton.* New York, 1915.

S.D.   stage direction

S.P.   speech prefix

Sugden   E. H. Sugden. *A Topographical Dictionary to the Works of Shakespeare and His Fellow Dramatists.* Manchester, 1925.

Tilley   Morris P. Tilley. *Dictionary of the Proverbs in England in the Sixteenth and Seventeenth Centuries.* Ann Arbor, 1950.

uncorr.   uncorrected

Woodall   John Woodall. *The Surgions Mate* . . . . London, 1617.

Introduction

THE TEXT

A Fair Quarrel was not originally entered in the Stationers' Register. However, the title page of the first quarto identifies the publisher:

A Faire Quarrell. As it was Acted before the King *and diuers times publikely by the* Prince his Highnes Seruants. Written by *Thomas Midleton* and *William Rowley.* Gentl. [Woodcut of the duellists in the play.] Printed at London for *I. T.* and are to bee sold at Christ Church Gate. 1617.

That "I.T." was John Trundle is confirmed by an entry in the Register for 2 September 1621 transferring *A Fair Quarrel* from John Trundle to Thomas Dewe. Trundle, then, was either part owner or sole owner of the copyright. But instead of his shop at the sign of Nobody, in the Barbican, the imprint of 1617 names the shop at Christ Church Gate (or Door) which had been given or sold by John Wright to his younger brother Edward Wright about the year 1615.[1] Therefore, Edward may have been co-owner of *A Fair Quarrel* in 1617.

Although the title page does not name the printer, bibliographical evidence in the quarto identifies him as George Eld, who printed a large number of plays in the years 1603 to 1620. Eld's compositors seem to have set *A Fair Quarrel* with more than average care; demonstrable errors, whether corrected at the press or left uncorrected, are remarkably few and textually

---

1. A bibliographical analysis of Q1 is to be found in my article, "The First Edition of *A Faire Quarrell*," *The Library*, 5th ser., 4 (1949): 137–41 (but I erred in saying on p. 140 that the running titles in the Additions had earlier been used in printing Q1). The entries of *A Fair Quarrel* in the Stationers' Register are given by W. W. Greg, *A Bibliography of the English Printed Drama to the Restoration,* 1 (London, 1939): 32, 36. See also 2 (London, 1951): 494–96.

insignificant.[2] The only other aspect of the printing to be noted here is that the preliminaries of the book were probably set last, as forme A1–2, after the text had been completed (its last quire being also a half-sheet, K1–2).[3] Though such a procedure was common, in this case it may have been followed to give Rowley time to compose the Epistle, if it had not been written when Trundle purchased the manuscript of the play.

The manuscript from which Q1 was set was almost certainly a fair copy prepared especially for the printer. Its original was probably the fair copy on which the promptbook was also based. That the promptbook itself served as copy is not likely; and still more implausible is the inference that the foul papers or another early draft was used by the printer. The dedication of *A Fair Quarrel* to Robert Gray, Groom of the Chamber to Prince Charles, alone would lead us to think Rowley or Rowley and Middleton had prepared the copy carefully. But much internal evidence leads to the same conclusion.

First of all, the entries and other stage directions are uniformly literary in wording, rather than theatrical. Other than the regular "Enter" formula, only one direction is in the imperative. The directions are nearly all in full (rather than abbreviated) and idiomatic form; for instance, "Exeunt Lady and her servants" and "Enter a friend of the Colonel's, and another of Captain Ager's." They are much more detailed than usual in play quartos; for example, "Offers to go away," "Reads his bill," and "Points to the Physician." Of about thirteen omitted stage directions which would have been helpful for a reader, only two are important, an entry and an exit; the rest are mostly asides. (Three asides are marked.) Another feature of the entries should be noted: out of a total of twenty-four which occur in the midst

2. The fourteen stop-press corrections in the text proper consisted of righting turned letters and similar changes. Nine are concentrated on the inner forme of sheet G, and the rest are scattered on the outer formes of B, D, E, and F. These variants are recorded in the textual notes of this edition. But I have omitted from the notes, as having no importance for the text, four corrections in three running titles and one signature; these variants occur in B2r, B4r, D4r, and I3r.

3. In brief, Q1 may be collated: [A1r], title page. [A1v], blank. A2r–[A2v], the epistle "To . . . Robert Grey." B1r, head title. B1r–[K2r], text. [K2v], blank.

of dialogue or soliloquy, nine are timed, that is, set a line or two ahead of the entering actor's first speech in order to allow him time to come down stage. On the other hand, fifteen are simultaneous, the entry being marked just before the actor's first line. A promptbook is distinguished, of course, by its timing of entries.

Other evidences of the authors' careful supervision of the text are the facts that there seems to have been no attempt to expunge profanity from the play; that although the spellings which help to distinguish the hands of the dramatists have been modified by the compositors, enough original spellings remain to suggest the authors' own writing in the manuscript; and that Q1 has few signs of corruption or omission in the text; possibly nothing has been lost except one or two stage directions. I believe that the handwriting of both authors appeared in the manuscript, and that Rowley himself edited it for the press.[4]

In summary, Q1 undoubtedly provides a fully authentic and, when compared to many other Jacobean editions of plays, an exceptionally correct text.

Bibliographically, the first edition of *A Fair Quarrel* exists in two issues. Issue 2 differs from the one described above in possessing a reset title page and a supplementary quire of three leaves inserted in the original quire H. These seven pages (the verso of the title leaf is blank) were all printed on one sheet, from which the new title leaf was cut off. When the remaining sheets of the edition were gathered to replenish Wright's stock of copies, the Issue 1 title leaf was cut off sheet A–K and the cancelling title leaf pasted in its place; at the same time, of course, the new three-leaved gathering was sewn in between the original H3 and H4 leaves. Hence in Issue 2 quire H is signed H1, H2, H3, H4, H3, [blank], H4.

The new title page omits the statement that the play had been acted publicly, in order to leave space for the advertisement of "new Additions of M^r. *Chaughs* and *Trimtrams* Roaring, and the Bauds Song." The date of 1617 is repeated. Assuming

---

4. For Middleton's habits of spelling, see my article, "The Early Editions of *A Trick to Catch the Old One*," *The Library*, 5th series, 22 (1967): 209–11. No analysis of Rowley's habits of spelling has been published; but I have studied the few surviving pieces of his holograph and the original editions of his unaided plays; see Appendix A below.

that when Rowley sold the manuscript with its dedication, the Additions had not yet been written, we infer that Issue 1 was printed during the first season of the play, perhaps in the early months of 1617. The supplementary farce must have been added for a revival in the late spring or early fall and the manuscript of the Additions then promptly sold to Trundle, for the unchanged date in Issue 2 shows that the publisher hoped to sell the rest of the copies within the year.

The textual importance, if any exists, of Issue 2 is solely in the Additions. Both bibliographical and stylistic evidence shows that these episodes were not part of the collaborated play as originally composed. Rather, they belong entirely to Rowley and were written to amplify the comic plot, in which he probably acted Trimtram, and which had apparently proved an unusual success. Because Middleton had no part in their conception or composition, the Additions are relegated to an appendix of this edition.

On 2 September 1621 John Trundle assigned his right in *A Fair Quarrel* to Thomas Dewe,[5] and near the end of 1621 or in 1622 Dewe republished the play with a title page which repeats that of Issue 2 of Q1 except for the imprint:

A Faire Quarrell. With new Additions . . . Written by *Thomas Midleton* and *William Rowley* . . . Printed at London by *A.M.* for *Thomas Dewe* and are to be sold at his shop in S. *Dunstones* Churchyard, in Fleetstreet. 1622.

Dewe had provided Augustine Mathewes, the printer, with a perfect copy of Issue 2, and accordingly, the Additions are incorporated without distinction into the text of Q2.

Corrections of Q1 by the printer of Q2 are few and unimportant; there is no sign of authorial intervention or of the printer's reference to a manuscript of the play. The basis of the text for modern editions must be Q1.

Only twelve copies (one completed with a manuscript section) of Q2 survive, a number small enough to suggest that the edition sold well and was widely read. Yet the stationers who

5. On the printing of Q2 see my article, "Compositors' Methods with Two Quartos Reprinted by Augustine Mathewes," *Papers of the Bibliographical Society of America*, 44 (1950): 269–72.

held copyright in the play after Dewe—John Helme, Helme's widow, and William Washington—did not publish it again. Alexander Dyce's edition, in *The Works of Thomas Middleton* (London, 1840) was the next one, upon which were based other nineteenth-century editions. Of twentieth-century ones those of Martin Sampson (*Thomas Middleton*, New York, 1915) and E. H. C. Oliphant (*Shakespeare and His Fellow Dramatists*, New York, 1921) are the most careful.

The present text is based on the collation of eleven copies of Q1, all that survive.[6] I have also collated two copies of Q2.

AUTHORSHIP

Though on the title page of Q1 Middleton's name comes first, it is Rowley who composes the dedication to Gray. The two facts probably cancel each other's implications about predominance of either man in the authorship. But Rowley's dedication may well have been an act of personal friendship with a special motive. Possibly Middleton voluntarily permitted his contribution to the play to be obscured by the dedication. Finally, then, in deciding the shares of the two writers we are left almost wholly to the evidence of style and structure and of spelling and other accidentals.

Analysis of the stylistic aspects is not easy, for *A Fair Quarrel* presents an admirable example of three actions neatly interwoven, the result, no doubt, of unusual care in planning and writing.[7] In distinguishing the writers' shares I have relied about equally on elements of diction, versification, and spelling, as well as on Middleton's propensity for irony and Rowley's obvious puns and love of absurd characterization.[8]

6. To Greg's list of ten (*Bibliography*, 2: 495) should be added a copy in the library of the University of Chicago.

7. This is the conclusion to be drawn from Richard Levin's analysis of the structure of the play in "The Three Quarrels of *A Fair Quarrel*," *Studies in Philology*, 41 (1964): 219–31.

8. Discussions of Rowley's style are to be found in studies by P. G. Wiggin, E. C. Morris, Dewar M. Robb, and others listed in the *Cambridge Bibliography of English Literature* (Cambridge, 1940) and *Supplement* (Cambridge, 1957), and in G. R. Price, "The Authorship and the Manuscript of *The Old Law*," *Huntington Library Quarterly*,

The scope of this Introduction permits only a statement of conclusions, not an exposition of the details upon which my ascription of each scene is based. However, as an example of the kinds of evidence used in the analysis of all the scenes, it may be pointed out that in Act I (which constitutes one scene) some of the signs of Rowley's composition (in addition to his handwriting in the printer's copy) are: (1) his habitual failure to make verse lines rhythmical, as, for instance, in these lines:

> . . . 'Tis not neatness
> Either in handsome wit or handsome outside,
> With which one gentleman, far in debt, has courted her,
> Which boldness he shall rue. He thinks me blind
> And ignorant; I have let him play a long time . . .
>
> (ll. 12–16)

(2) the appearance of such words as "tush," "humh," "brabling," and "propagation," which are often repeated in his unaided plays and occur in this act; (3) his usual spellings, e.g., *um* for *them* (Middleton spells it *e'm*) and the preterite endings -*'d* and -*d* (Middleton commonly uses -*de*, sometimes -*d*); (4) the constant and obvious puns so typical of Rowley, for instance, on *but*, line 119; (5) the allusion in lines 333–34 to the great frost of 1608, which Rowley mentions again in his tract, *A Search for Money* (1609); and parallels with his play *A Woman Never Vexed* (ca. 1620)—notably a heroine named Jane, daughter of a rich merchant, and her prodigal lover who is kept in debtors' prison.

From such evidence it may be inferred that, after careful planning of the scenario by both partners, Rowley himself wrote Act I (421 lines).

Act II is divided into two scenes. The first, showing Ager with his mother and his friends, is by Middleton (248 lines). The second, of the Physician's intrigue and Chough's discussion of roaring, is Rowley's (235 lines). Act III is in three episodes. The first, of the duel, is Middleton's work (183 lines); the second,

---

16 (1953): 117–39. My ascription of scenes in *A Fair Quarrel* corresponds exactly to that of E. H. C. Oliphant, *Shakespeare and His Fellow Dramatists*, 2 (New York, 1929): 804–49.

continuing the Physician's intrigue, is by Rowley (175 lines); and the third, of Lady Ager's anguish, is again by Middleton (44 lines). Act IV has three scenes also. First is one of the roaring school, by Rowley (227 lines). In Scene ii the Colonel's Sister talks first with the Surgeon, then with his patient, the Colonel; this is all by Middleton (119 lines). In Scene iii, also by Middleton, Ager meets his mother again and then accepts the Colonel's Sister as bride (124 lines). Although not divided into scenes, Act V has two parts, first, the resolution of the Physician's intrigue and of Russell's against Fitzallen, and, second, the reconciliation of Ager and the Colonel. The former (385 lines) is Rowley's, the latter (55 lines) Middleton's.

If the preceding ascriptions are correct, the total of lines (773) which Middleton contributed to the play amounts to 34.8%. Unquestionably this percentage fails to gauge the importance of his help in creating the scenario, individualizing the characters, and developing the theme. It is obvious that the playwrights agreed upon a basic division of their project, namely, Rowley's composition of an intrigue borrowed from a novella and farced with topical humor about roaring boys, to be combined with Middleton's description of the passions roused by a conflict in Renaissance conceptions of honor, a conflict presented in realistic terms. It is quite certain, therefore, that from the dramatists' point of view, as from our own, Middleton's contribution was not less important than Rowley's.

THE DATE OF COMPOSITION AND PRODUCTION

The dates of composition and production of *A Fair Quarrel* are not mentioned in any known document, and we have to infer what we can from internal evidence, chiefly topical references in the text. These are not conclusive, but they point rather clearly to 1616, the date traditionally assigned.

Perhaps the more precise of two references to contemporary problems is made by the two sergeants' use of the disguise of diggers of saltpeter. The other contemporary interest is a major element in the play, that of honor and the private duel. Both matters were popular concerns long before 1616. With respect to the former, public opposition to the entrance of diggers upon private lands had caused legal problems for decades, notably in 1603 and 1607. In 1616 the saltpeter men complained of being unable to rent carts from anyone; their work was so much hampered that the resulting scarcity of gunpowder spurred the Privy Council to force the public to cooperate with the diggers. Although the Council's order was issued on 22 May 1617, the crisis had probably arisen about a year earlier.

The theme of honor and the duel had also become a public concern even before James I's accession. In a letter of 9 September 1613 John Chamberlain cited six recent challenges and duels. In 1614 Sir Francis Bacon prosecuted the case of Priest and Wright in Star Chamber; his charge to the Court was ordered by the King to be published as expressing his own views, which were reinforced by James's proclamation against challenges on 4 February 1614. In 1616 Gervase Markham's challenge of Lord Darcy of the North resulted in another prosecution in Star Chamber.[9] However, no particular combat, merely the public's general interest in duelling, is reflected in *A Fair Quarrel*.

Therefore, it is possible that the play was written in 1615 or even earlier. But in view of the popular resistance to saltpeter diggers in 1616, it seems more likely that the play's first season was the fall and winter of 1616–17. The Additions were probably also on the stage by the late spring or early fall of 1617. We have noted above that the printing of both issues of Q1 probably took place during the first nine or ten months of that year. Rowley's promptness in publishing seems to ask for an explanation, but only a conjecture can be offered. Rowley was made a member of the Duke of York's Men in 1609, in which year also a truce in the Low Countries brought home many soldiers, among them,

9. References to the troubles in digging saltpeter are scattered through the *Calendar of State Papers Domestic Series . . . 1603–1610* (London, 1857), e.g., p. 356, and through *Acts of the Privy Council, 1616–1617* (London, 1890), e.g., pp. 47–48, 132–33. The significance of the allusion in *A Fair Quarrel* was first mentioned by M. W. Sampson, *Thomas Middleton* (New York, 1915), p. 202.

Fredson Bowers, in "Middleton's *Fair Quarrel* and the Duelling Code," *Journal of English and Germanic Philology*, 36 (1937): 40–65, cites many notorious combats. For the two mentioned here, see *The Charge of Sir Francis Bacon Knight . . . against Priest and Wright* (1614), sig. H2r, and *The Reports of . . . Sr Henry Hobart . . . Lord Chief Justice . . . The Fourth Edition* (1678), sig. R1r.

no doubt, Robert Gray. This man, to whom Rowley dedicates the work, was a member of an eminent Scottish family; in 1604 King James had recommended him for command of a company in the army of the Estates General. In 1609, having returned to London, Gray received a free gift of £800. By 1610 he was one of the Grooms of the Bedchamber to Prince Charles. In 1612/13 he was granted, by courtesy, the M.A. from Cambridge University when the Prince visited there.[10]

It can hardly be doubted that Rowley and Gray became acquainted in 1609 when both were made servants of the Prince. Gray was about thirty-six, probably nearly ten years older than Rowley, and much more widely experienced. Perhaps the soldier had some interest in the theater. It is even possible to detect in the Epistle a hint that Gray suggested the theme of the play. Rowley seems to have admired him and to have interested Middleton in him and in the problem of honor. I have found no record of a conflict like Captain Ager's with the Colonel in *A Fair Quarrel*. But possibly one of Gray's anecdotes furnished a basis for the plot; and it seems quite likely that Rowley intended his readers to understand *Ager* as an anagram of *Grey*, as the name is spelled in the Epistle.[11]

Certainly one understands from the Epistle that the play was a success. Wishing to capitalize as much as possible on the success, Rowley brought the play into print with unusual haste. It is to be hoped that Captain Gray was generous at once, for his relation with Rowley must have ended a year or so after the publication. His name does not appear again in English

10. James Ferguson, ed., *Papers Illustrating the History of the Scots Brigade in the Service of the United Netherlands 1572–1782*, 1 (Edinburgh, 1899): 193–94; J. Nichols, *The Progresses . . . of King James the First*, 2 (London, 1828), 288; E. Turnor, "A Declaration of the Diet and particular Fare of K. Charles the First, when Duke of York," *Archaeologia*, 15 (1806): 8; John and J. A. Venn, *The Book of Matriculations and Degrees . . . in the University of Cambridge* (Cambridge, 1913), pp. xxvi, 299.

11. *Gray*, the spelling adopted for the Epistle in this edition, was traditional for the Scottish family; see the works cited in notes 10 and 12. However, *Grey*, the spelling for such English families as the Greys of Ruthyn, Groby, Merton, and Werke, was doubtless far more familiar to Rowley and the readers of the quarto.

records; between 1617 and 1621 he seems to have married a Scots widow and to have settled down permanently in Scotland.[12]

The contemporary stage history of *A Fair Quarrel*, apart from the inferences made above, is confined to two notices. Papers from the Office of the Revels show that this play was considered for performance at Court in 1619 or 1620, and perhaps it was performed. There is also a record of a production by Beeston's Boys on 10 August 1639.[13]

THE SOURCES

Other than a conjectural anecdote of Captain Gray's, the sources of *A Fair Quarrel* are two stories identified by Gerard Langbaine in 1691.[14] The two, both in the genre of the novella, are combined by Rowley in the ordeals of Jane and Fitzallen. One story is Cinthio Giraldi's and is taken from *Hecatommithi*, Decade 4, Novella 5; it recounts a Physician's lust for an Italian girl, with very exact counterparts for Jane, Anne, and the Dutch Nurse; it differs by ending in severe punishment for the Physician. The other story, found by Langbaine in *The Complaisant Companion* (1674), was probably read by Rowley in an earlier English jest book, although its origin may have been Continental. It tells of a rich citizen's daughter who has secretly married a country gentleman. When her parents become aware of her pregnancy and learn the identity of her fiancé (she asserts that there has been a promise of marriage), they negotiate with the gentleman about the dowry and finally offer a good one. The secret marriage is then revealed, and the relieved father even adds to the dowry.

Rowley varies from this story by having Russell imprison Fitzallen by a trick, then release him in hope of deceiving him into accepting a baby of unknown paternity along with a dishonored wife. To cap all this, Russell, after learning the truth,

12. Sir James Balfour Paul, ed., *The Scots Peerage*, 4 (Edinburgh, 1907): 80, 89. References to Robert Gray of Cranneslie, whom I take to be the former Groom, are scattered through the Scottish state papers, mostly in connection with legal business.

13. Gerald Eades Bentley, *The Jacobean and Caroline Stage*, 1 (Oxford, 1941): 215.

14. *An Account of the English Dramatick Poets*, 1691, sig. Aa2v.

tries to reduce the dowry by a thousand pounds! Citizen Russell's baseness contrasts to the idealistic generosity of the repentant Colonel, as well as to Captain Ager's nobility. In this connection it may be noted that the Additions provide a further contrast to Ager and the Colonel. Captain Arthur Severus O'Toole, a notorious braggart and pimp then living in London, is lampooned in the Additions and is another instance of the degradation to which soldiers might sink, in the way in which the master and usher of the roaring school have done.[15]

THE THEME

Before making a critical appraisal of *A Fair Quarrel* it is necessary to state certain features of the code of honor and of the protocol of the private duel which have been omitted by previous commentators on this play.

At the end of the sixteenth century the theory of honor was often discussed in print by English preachers, lawyers, moralists, courtiers, and ex-soldiers. From their expositions one sees that the quarrel between Ager and the Colonel involves both native (or imperfect) and acquired (or perfect) honor. Native honor, an attribute of gentle birth, remains with a man unless he loses it by an act of cowardice or untruth or by a failure to act in defense of his reputation for valor and justice. But when he loses native honor, he also loses whatever acquired honor has accrued to him for his feats of arms or statesmanlike service of his prince. "[There can]not be honour acquired, where there is not honor natural," says Sir John Kepers.[16] Therefore, when the Colonel impugns Lady Ager's virtue, by the same words he calls Ager a bastard; and we perceive how much is at stake for the Captain. If he does not immediately refute the charge with his sword, his father's, his mother's, and his own honor are all lost, including the glory he has recently won by remarkable feats of valor in battle. Henceforth no gentleman need respect him, his career as

15. John Taylor, in *The Great O'Toole*, 1622, a mock eulogy, complains that returned soldiers have to become highwaymen, tobacco merchants, pimps, and panders; but he credits O'Toole with having been a soldier, whereas Albo is a mere imposter (sigs. A6v, B1r).

16. *The Courtiers Academie . . . Originally written in Italian by Count Haniball Romei*, 1598(?), sig. M2v.

an officer will be blighted, and no advantageous marriage will be possible. (We can grant that these disastrous consequences are described as more inevitable in the theory of honor than we find them to have been in actual life, without thereby reducing their importance in the drama; for the very frequency of duels proves the acceptance of the theory.)

In this context we must also bear in mind the enormity of the Colonel's crime, apart from its wrong to the Ager family. The Colonel is a proud, wrathy man; the angry words for which, after time for reflection, he should have asked pardon, he chooses to defend in defiance of the God of truth and at the risk of eternal salvation. "For hee that persisteth to maintaine evill doth condemne himselfe, as a man that would fight contrary to justice . . . rather a beast than a Christian, and a furious foole . . . ."[17] The theme of the play has as a datum that a private duel must be considered a trial by combat, in which God awards victory to the man fighting for truth. Having slandered Lady Ager, the Colonel tempts God by defending the slander. Ager's integrity in refusing to defend a falsehood (i.e., in refusing to try to vindicate his mother's purity and honor which, as he now believes, she lost long ago) contrasts absolutely to the Colonel's depravity; see II.i.207–10. In fact, it is the very heinousness of the Colonel's guilt which helps to make plausible his final repentance and his amends.

The scene (III.i) in which Ager, meeting the Colonel on the field of honor, tries to reconcile his opponent, is handled by Middleton with great psychological and dramatic skill; yet the significance of Ager's behavior is slightly obscured if we ignore elements of the code of honor. Lady Ager's confession, which is understood by the audience as a lie, a ruse to keep her son from the combat, has deprived him in conscience of the right to fight. In Ager's view the Colonel's insult merely publicized Lady Ager's offense; though the Colonel, in his anger, may only have thought he was using a formula of provocation, nevertheless he spoke the truth. However, he is guilty of a cruel sin against charity, detraction. If he can be induced to withdraw the insult, the honor of the Agers will be restored, in the narrow sense of

17. Sir William Segar, *The Booke of Honor and Armes*, 1590, sigs. G4v–H1r.

honor basic to the code, that is, a reputation that has never been openly challenged. Since the Colonel has been Ager's friend and certainly has heard of Lady Ager's virtuous widowhood, his repentance and retraction of the insult seem possible. This much the Captain wishes to accomplish for his mother's sake. As for himself, "I should be dead, for all my life's work's ended" (II.i.207). His career as gentleman and officer is ruined because he knows of her dishonor.

Speaking to the Colonel in this belief (III.i.70–89) and determined not to fight, Ager is, of course, using some concealment; he is pretending to possess honor, for he does not admit the truth of the Colonel's words. But the audience, sharing his anguish and knowing that in fact the Colonel's words were slander, of course do not want Ager to avow his mother's dishonor, and they are hardly conscious of his duplicity. And Ager's urging of a Christian desire for peace and friendship is unquestionably sincere (ll. 70–72); this is proved, first, by his love of truth, shown in his refusal to fight for a falsehood; second, by his mild, conciliatory attitude at Russell's house (I.i); and third, by his religious consideration of the damnation that falls on a man who dies while pursuing revenge (ll. 81–87). At the end of his speech, Ager gently hints that the Colonel may admit to having spoken without knowledge (ll. 88–89). But the Colonel is unconcerned about the truth of his insult; he has used it only as a means to revenge himself upon Ager for the Captain's exasperating comparison of their valors and for Fitzallen's disgrace by Russell (I.i) and in order to force Ager into combat. In the Colonel's view of the code of honor, to withdraw the insult would be to dishonor himself.

Whether Ager is technically the Challenger in this duel, as Fredson Bowers believes,[18] or whether he is Defender (the giving of the lie having been understood), does not materially affect our view of his behavior. It was considered more appropriate for the Defender (the party first injured) to make overtures for peace; but in any case the attempt must be made before the enemies come to the field. Therefore, Ager's unconventional (and humiliating) endeavor to conciliate the Colonel on the field

18. "Middleton's *Fair Quarrel* and the Duelling Code," *Journal of English and Germanic Philology*, 36 (1937), 49, 60–62.

more strikingly reveals his fidelity to moral truth in honor. But he can accomplish his purpose only by inducing the Colonel to use phraseology that admits having made an error. The word "pardon" must not be introduced, for it implies superiority in one party or the other; "some fallation [must] be used," says Kepers. Inadvertently Ager speaks the words "pardon" and "repentance," and the Colonel's anger is renewed. He hurls a new insult, "coward," which Ager knows he can truthfully repel. However, this second insult is not the result of guileful provocation by Ager. Such trickery would be inconsistent with his dominant characteristic, strict fidelity to the truth.

Yet Middleton, whether for momentary dramatic effect or for realism, allows some inconsistency to blur Ager's principles. Believing himself to be a man without honor, and having refused to fight for a falsehood, Ager now challenges and defeats a man at least technically honorable—although earlier Ager has lamented that never again would he have use for valor (II.i.203). His preceding attempt to draw an apology from the Colonel is likewise a descent to the protection of a fallacious convention. But this oscillation between two conceptions of morality does not really vitiate the characterization of Ager, for the mundane view of honor only generates a part of his emotion, whereas strict integrity governs his deeds. Furthermore, although the law of arms dictated that the seconds should forbid this duel because Ager has lost all honor by failing to fight on the first charge or challenge, instead, the seconds give full sanction to the combat, as very frequently happened in reality. Therefore, the title of the play has no irony; Ager's quarrel is fair and his appeal to arms is as just as anyone in his world can ask (III.i.160–61). His victory is a double vindication, although he does not know it at the time. He leaves his enemy almost at the point of death. There is little cause for surprise in the Colonel's immediate change of heart.

One more point of the code is to be noted. Although Ager fails to demand the spoils due to the victor—the weapons, armor, garments, even the person of his enemy—the repentant Colonel acknowledges Ager's right, as well as the recompense due for violated friendship and the restitution to be made for grievous moral wrong. Hence he delivers his property, and even his sister, to Ager. The ideas of ransom and restitution are fused.

While concerned with the theory of honor and the duel, the preceding statements have inevitably touched on vital moral forces moving the action of the play. Though other aspects of the moral truth of Ager's situation must be left unmentioned here, it should be said that Middleton's usual finesse in handling this kind of motivation is present. For instance, one observes that Ager's scruple about fighting without absolute assurance of his mother's purity (perhaps the major flaw in the play's realism) finds its solution in a lie which attributes to the Colonel the defense of Lady Ager against the insult offered by another man. Ager's falsehood is caused by his fear of her anger, as well as by unwarranted doubt of her purity; and it meets swift punishment by her falsehood of self-accusation. She later acknowledges that her lie has brought its appropriate punishment. But the Captain's youthful egoism seems to prevent his discerning any fitness in the consequence of his lie.

Rowley, also, has managed to give a general validity of psychological and moral truth to the plot of Russell and the lovers. Though softened a little by his notable tenderness for his daughter, Russell's cunning and avarice are appropriately frustrated by the constancy of the lovers and by the Physician's contemptuous miscalculation of Chough's stupidity. More important critically than Rowley's good manipulation of this plot is the matter of his intention and accomplishment in introducing the novella-story and the farce of Chough and Trimtram into the drama of Captain Ager's ordeal. The purpose of mingling these elements has been analyzed by Richard Levin in an article which every student of the play should read.[19] The following comments are intended to modify Levin's insistence on "honor" as the key idea in the play.

Jane's honor is real purity, which she protects against the treachery of both her father and the Physician. Strengthened by her own love and courage and by her lover's, she finds an unexpected ally in the Physician's sister and some accidental help from Chough. What Jane defends is essential virtue within her marriage (the precontract). Ager, however, has another kind of good to defend, an external one, yielded to him by others; yet it is

19. See Note 7 above.

dependent on his deliberate action according to his conscience and a code of rules. The ruling virtue of both characters may more properly be called "fortitude" than "honor": Jane is staunch in devotion to purity and troth-plight, Ager in devotion to truth (while agonizing over worldly honor). The term "honor" does not, therefore, provide the clue to the interrelated meaning of the three plots. The dramatists intended a more general contrast of morality in several social types.

Ager is the pattern of soldierly behavior, the man of honor who has harmonized the social code with moral truth. The Colonel and Russell contrast impressively to Ager, for throughout most of the play both are devoid of conscience (Russell never attains it). The soldiers of the roaring school are men of honor degenerated into cheats. Chough, a boor, is as far from Ager's conception of honor as he is from decorum of manners or real virtue. These seem to me to be the significant contrasts intended by the dramatists. Aesthetically, that is, dramatically, they emphasize the thesis of the play, that duels would be very rare if men of all classes were governed by as religious a conscience as Ager's. Such a view of the devotion to honor as a worldly good may be too simplistic; but it does not "smudge the issues between wrong and right," as a respected critic once asserted.[20] And it accounts for the Prince's Men daring to present at Court a play that seems, on the surface, to glorify duelling.

GEORGE R. PRICE

Michigan State University

20. Muriel C. Bradbrook, *Themes and Conventions of Elizabethan Tragedy* (Cambridge, 1935), p. 72.

A FAIR QUARREL

To the Nobly Disposed, Virtuous, and Faithful-Breasted
Robert Gray, Esquire, One of the Grooms of His High-
ness's Bed-Chamber, His Poor Well-Willer Wisheth His
Best Wishes, *Hic et Supra*.

WORTHY SIR,   5

    'Tis but a play, and a play is but a butt against which
many shoot many arrows of envy. 'Tis the weaker part,
and how much more noble shall it be in you to defend
it! Yet if it be (as some philosophers have left behind
'em) that this megacosm, this great world, is no more than   10
a stage where everyone must act his part, you shall
of necessity have many part-takers, some long, some
short, some indifferent, all some; whilst indeed the
players themselves have the least part of it; for I know
few that have lands (which are a part of the world)   15
and therefore no grounded men. But, howsoever, they
serve for mutes; happily they must wear good clothes
for attendance, yet all have exits and must all be stripp'd
in the tiring house (viz. the grave), for none must carry
anything out of the stock. You see, sir, I write as I   20
speak, and I speak as I am, and that's excuse enough for
me. I did not mean to write an epistle of praise to you;
it looks so like a thing I know you love not, flattery,
which you exceedingly hate actively and unpleasingly

2. *Robert Gray*] See the Introduction, pp. xviii-xx.
2–3. *His Highness's*] Charles was created Prince of Wales 4 November 1616. See Introduction, p. xviii, with regard to the short interval
between the first production and the printing of this play.
4. *Hic et Supra*] "on this occasion, as formerly."
6. *butt*] in archery the mound or structure on which the target
was set.
7. *'Tis . . . part*] The play is the weaker party in its contest with
the public.
9. *some philosophers*] e.g., Plato *The Laws* 1.644de and 7.803c, and
John of Salisbury, *Policraticus*, Book 3, chaps. 8 and 9.
17. *happily*] with a pun on "haply," on occasion.

accept passively. Indeed, I meant to tell you your own, 25
that is, that this child of the Muses is yours; whoever
begot it, 'tis laid to your charge, and, for aught I know,
you must father and keep it, too. If it please you, I
hope you shall not be asham'd of it, neither; for it has
been seen, though I say it, in good companies, and many 30
have said it is a handsome, pretty-spoken infant. Now be
your own judge; at your leisure look on it, at your pleasure laugh at it, and if you be sorry it is no better, you
may be glad it is no bigger.

Yours ever, 35

WILLIAM ROWLEY

25. *tell . . . own*] Possibly Gray proposed the theme to the playwrights, or one of his experiences suggested it to them.

[CHARACTERS OF THE PLAY

CAPTAIN AGER, *son of Lady Ager*
THE COLONEL
TWO FRIENDS OF AGER
TWO FRIENDS OF THE COLONEL
RUSSELL, *brother of Lady Ager, a rich merchant*   5
FITZALLEN, *kinsman of the Colonel*
CHOUGH, *a Cornish gentleman*
TRIMTRAM, *Chough's man*
A PHYSICIAN
A SURGEON   10
VAPOR, *a tobacco-seller*
TWO SERGEANTS, *bailiffs in one of the law-courts*
AN USHER *in the Roaring School, an ex-soldier*
SECOND ROARER, *another ex-soldier*
SERVANTS *to Russell and Lady Ager*   15

LADY AGER, *a widow*
JANE, *daughter of Russell*
THE COLONEL'S SISTER
ANNE, *sister of the Physician, a midwife*
A DUTCH NURSE]   20

4. Friends . . . Colonel] One of these is master of the Roaring School and therefore "first roarer" (IV.i.1–3); the other is the Colonel's companion (V.i.407–8). They serve as the Colonel's seconds (III.i.45.1).

A Fair Quarrel

Enter Master Russell *solus.*

RUSSELL.

    It must be all my care; there's all my love,
And that pulls on the tother. Had I been left
In a son behind me, while I had been here
He should have shifted as I did before him,
Liv'd on the freeborn portion of his wit.   5
But a daughter, and that an only one—oh!
We cannot be too careful o' her, too tender!
'Tis such a brittle niceness, a mere cupboard of glasses;
The least shake breaks or cracks 'em. All my aim is
To cast her upon riches. That's the thing   10
We rich men call perfection, for the world
Can perfect naught without it. 'Tis not neatness
Either in handsome wit or handsome outside,
With which one gentleman, far in debt, has courted her,
Which boldness he shall rue. He thinks me blind   15
And ignorant; I have let him play a long time,
Seem'd to believe his worth, which I know nothing.
He may perhaps laugh at my easy confidence,
Which closely I requite upon his fondness.
For this hour snaps him; and before his mistress,   20
His saint, forsooth, which he inscribes my girl,
He shall be rudely taken and disgrac'd.
The trick will prove an everlasting scarecrow
To fright poor gallants from our rich men's daughters.

    Enter the Lady Ager, *with two servants.*

---

2. *that . . . tother*] "My love arouses my concern."
8. *niceness*] tendency to foolishness or wantonness.
19. *Which*] refers to the idea of laughter.

Sister! I've such a joy to make you a welcome of;   25
Better you never tasted.
LADY AGER.   Good sir, spare it not.
RUSSELL.
Colonel's come, and your son Captain Ager.
LADY AGER.
My son!   *She weeps.*
RUSSELL.   I know your eye would be first serv'd;
That's the soul's taster still for grief or joy.
LADY AGER.
Oh, if a mother's dear suit may prevail with him,   30
From England he shall never part again.
RUSSELL.
No question he'll be rul'd, and grant you that.
LADY AGER.
I'll bring all my desires to that request.
                              Exeunt Lady *and her servants.*
RUSSELL.
Affectionate sister! she has no daughter now;
It follows all the love must come to him,   35
And he has a worth deserves it, were it dearer.

Enter a Friend of the Colonel *and a* Friend of Captain Ager.

COLONEL'S FRIEND.
I must not give way to't.
RUSSELL [*aside*].   What's here to question?
COLONEL'S FRIEND.
Compare young Captain Ager with the Colonel!
AGER'S FRIEND.
Young? Why, do you make youth stand for an imputa-
    tion?
That which you now produce for his disgrace   40
Infers his nobleness, that, being young,
Should have an anger more inclin'd to courage
And moderation than the Colonel;

41–48. *that . . . for*] Ironically, this description of Ager's disciplined
character is spoken by a gentleman, probably an officer, who is typi-
cally rash in defense of honor. (See Matthew Sutcliffe, *The Practice,
Proceedings, and Lawes of armes*, 1593, sig.Xx3v.)

A virtue as rare as chastity in youth.
And let the cause be good—conscience in him   45
Which ever crowns his acts, and is indeed
Valor's prosperity—he dares then as much
As ever made him famous that you plead for.
COLONEL'S FRIEND.

Then I forbear too long.
AGER'S FRIEND.   His worth for me.   [*They draw.*]
RUSSELL.

Here's noble youths! Belike some wench has cross'd 'em,   50
And now they know not what to do with their blood.

Enter the Colonel *and* Captain Ager.

COLONEL.

How now!
CAPTAIN AGER.   Hold, hold, what's the incitement?
COLONEL.

So serious at your game! Come, come, the quarrel?
COLONEL'S FRIEND.

Nothing, good faith, sir.
COLONEL.   Nothing? And you bleed?
COLONEL'S FRIEND.

Bleed, where? Pish, a little scratch by chance, sir.   55
COLONEL.

What need this niceness, when you know so well
That I must know these things, and truly know 'em?
Your daintiness makes me but more impatient;
This strange concealment frets me.
COLONEL'S FRIEND.   Words did pass
Which I was bound to answer, as my opinion   60
And love instructed me; and should I take in general fame
Into 'em, I think I should commit no error in't.
COLONEL.

What words, sir, and of whom?
COLONEL'S FRIEND.   This gentleman
Parallel'd Captain Ager's worth with yours.

48. made] *Q2;* mad *Q1.*

—9—

COLONEL.

 With mine!

COLONEL'S FRIEND.   It was a thing I could not listen to   65
 With any patience.

CAPTAIN AGER.   What should ail you, sir?
 There was little wrong done to your friend i'that.

COLONEL.

 How! Little wrong, to me?

CAPTAIN AGER.   I said so, friend,
 And I suppose that you'll esteem it so.

COLONEL.

 Comparisons?

CAPTAIN AGER.   Why, sir, twixt friend and friend   70
 There is so even and level a degree
 It will admit of no superlative.

COLONEL.

 Not in terms of manhood?

RUSSELL [coming forward].   Nay, gentlemen—

COLONEL.

 Good, sir, give me leave—in terms of manhood?
 What can you dispute more questionable?   75
 You are a captain, sir; I give you all your due.

CAPTAIN AGER.

 And you are a colonel, a title
 Which may include within it many captains;
 Yet, sir, but throwing by those titular shadows,
 Which add no substance to the men themselves,   80
 And take them uncompounded, man and man,
 They may be so with fair equality.

COLONEL.

 Y'are a boy, sir!

CAPTAIN AGER.   And you have a beard, sir.
 Virginity and marriage are both worthy,

65. not] Q2; nor Q1.   73. S.D. coming forward] Dyce;
70. Comparisons] Q2; Compati-   not in Q1–2.
sons Q1.

78. many captains] A colonel commanded a regiment made up of
several companies, each under its captain who chose his lieutenants and
other lower officers (Sutcliffe, Practice, sig.L3r.)

<pre>
                                                            85
</pre>

And the positive purity there are some   85
Have made the nobler.

COLONEL.   How now?

RUSSELL.   Nay, good sir—

CAPTAIN AGER.
    I shrink not; he that goes the foremost
    May be o'ertaken.

COLONEL.   Death, how am I weighed!

CAPTAIN AGER.
    In an even balance, sir, a beard put in
    Gives but a small advantage; man and man,   '90
    And lift the scales.

COLONEL.   Patience shall be my curse
    If it ride me further!

RUSSELL.   How now, gallants?
    Believe me then, I must give aim no longer.
    Can words beget swords and bring 'em forth, ha?
    Come, they are abortive propagations;   95
    Hide 'em for shame! I had thought soldiers
    Had been musical, would not strike out of time,
    But to the consort of drum, trumps, and fife.
    'Tis madman-like to dance without music,
    And most unpleasing shows to the beholders,   100
    A Lydian ditty to a Doric note.
    Friends embrace with steel hands? Fie, it meets too hard!
    I must have those encounters here debarr'd.

COLONEL.
    Shall I lose here what I have safe brought home
    Through many dangers?

CAPTAIN AGER.   What's that, sir?

COLONEL.   My fame,   105
    Life of the life, my reputation.

102. hard] *Q1 (corr.); on l. 103 in
Q1 (uncorr.).*

105–6. *My . . . reputation*] "There is nothing so powerfull to
prostitute the heroicall mind to all vanitie, as an ouergood conceit of
a mans owne worthines . . . . that pride . . . breaketh oftentimes
foorth into cursed enuie, the inuisible roote . . . of execrable euills"
(John Norden, *The Mirror of Honor*, 1597, sigs. D4v–E1r).

Death! I am squar'd and measur'd out; my heights,
Depths, breadth, all my dimensions taken!
Sure I have yet beyond your astrolabe
A spirit unbounded.

CAPTAIN AGER.   Sir, you might weigh—

RUSSELL.   Tush,   110
All this is weighing fire, vain and fruitless;
The further it runs into argument,
The further plung'd; beseech you, no more on't.
I have a little claim, sir, in your blood,
As near as the brother to your mother;   115
If that may serve for power to move your quiet,
The rest I shall make up with courtesy
And an uncle's love.

CAPTAIN AGER.   I have done sir, but—

RUSSELL.

But! I'll have no more shooting at these butts.

COLONEL.

We'll to pricks when he please.

RUSSELL.   You rove all still.   120
Sir, I have no motive proof to disgest
Your rais'd choler back into temperate blood;
But if you'll make mine age a counsellor—
As all ages have hitherto allow'd it,
Wisdom in men grows up as years increase—   125
You shall make me blessed in making peace,
And do your judgment right.

110–11. Tush/ All] *Dyce; one*
line in Q1–2.

---

111. *weighing fire*] proverbial for futile endeavor (Tilley, F 288).
120. *pricks*] the target proper, or bull's eye (with a quibble on "swords").
120. *rove*] shoot at marks selected at random, in order to gain practice in judging distance (hence the idea of inexactness or being mistaken).
121–22. *disgest . . . blood*] Disgest is another form of "digest." Choler (bile) was believed to be formed in the liver and to issue from it with the blood; the heat of anger raises the lighter choler up to the heart, thus increasing incipient passion (Lawrence Babb, *The Elizabethan Malady* [East Lansing, Mich.,1951], pp. 6, 13–15).

COLONEL.   In peace at home
  Grey hairs are senators; but to determine
  Soldiers and their actions—

              Enter Fitzallen *and* Jane.

RUSSELL.   'Tis peace here, sir,
  And see, here comes a happy interim.   130
  Here enters now a scene of loving arms;
  This couple will not quarrel so.
COLONEL'S FRIEND.   Be advis'd, sir;
  This gentleman, Fitzallen, is your kinsman;
  You may o'erthrow his long labor'd fortunes
  With one angry minute. 'Tis a rich churl,   135
  And this his sole inheritrix; blast not
  His hopes with this tempest.
COLONEL.   It shall calm me;
  All the town's conjurors and their demons
  Could not have laid my spirit so.
FITZALLEN.   Worthy coz,
  I gratulate your fair return to peace.   140
  Your swift fame was at home long before you.
COLONEL.
  It meets, I hope, your happy fortunes here,
  And I am glad in't. I must salute your joys, coz,
  With a soldier's encounter.   *Kisses her.*
FITZALLEN.   Worthy Captain Ager!
  I hope my kinsman shortly.
RUSSELL [*aside*].   You must come short indeed, 145
  Or the length of my device will be ill shrunk.—
  Why, now it shows finely. I'll tell you, sir—
  Sir? nay, son; I know i'th'end 'twill be so—
FITZALLEN.
  I hope so, sir.
RUSSELL.   Hope? Nay, 'tis past all hope, son—

---

135. *churl*] niggard, miser.
146. *length . . . ill shrunk*] "My effort will fall miserably short of its intended effect."
147. *it . . . finely*] probably "the weather's fair now."

Here has been such a stormy encounter   150
Betwixt my cousin Captain and this brave Colonel
About I know not what—nothing indeed;
Competitions, degrees, and comparatives
Of soldiership; but this smooth passage
Of love has calm'd it all. Come, I'll have't sound;   155
Let me see your hearts combined in your hands,
And then I will believe the league is good.
It shall be the grape's if we drink any blood.

COLONEL.

   I have no anger, sir.

CAPTAIN AGER.   I have had none;
My blood has not yet rose to a quarrel.   160
Nor have you had cause.

COLONEL.   No cause of quarrel?
Death! If my father should tell me so—

RUSSELL.   Again!

FITZALLEN.

Good sir, for my sake!

COLONEL.   Faith, I have done, coz;
You do too hastily believe mine anger.
And yet to say diminuting valor   165
In a soldier is no cause of quarrel!

RUSSELL.

Nay, then, I'll remove the cause to kill th'effect.
Kinsman, I'll press you to't, if either love
Or consanguinity may move you to't;
I must disarm you, though ye are a soldier.   170
Pray, grant me your weapon; it shall be safe
At your regress from my house; now I know
No words can move this noble soldier's sword
To a man undefens'd so. We shall parle,
And safely make all perfect friends again.   175

COLONEL.

To show my will, sir, accept mine to you;
As good not wear it as not dare to use it.

---

165. *diminuting*] "lessening, belittling." (*OED* marks this verb
"rare" and does not record the *deminiting* of *Q1–2*.)

COLONEL'S FRIEND.

    Nay, then, sir, we will be all exampled.

    We'll have no arms here now but lovers' arms.

AGER'S FRIEND.

    No seconds must begin a quarrel; take mine, sir.   180

RUSSELL.

    Why, law, what a fine sun shines here! These clouds

    My breath has blown into another climate.

    I'll be your armorers; they are not pawn'd.—

    [*Aside.*] These were the fish that I did angle for.

    I have caught 'em finely; now for my trick.   185

    My project's lusty and will hit the nick. *Exit with weapons.*

COLONEL.

    What, is't a match, beauty? I would now have

    Alliance with my worthy Captain Ager,

    To knit our loves the faster; here's witness

    Enough if you confirm it now.

JANE.   Sir, my voice   190

    Was long since given, since that I gave my hand.

COLONEL.

    Would you had seal'd too.

JANE [*aside*].   That wish comes too late,

    For I too soon fear my delivery.—

    My father's hand sticks yet, sir. You may now

    Challenge a lawful interest in his;   195

    He took your hand from your enraged blood

    And gave it freely to your opposite,

    My cousin Ager. Methinks you should claim from him,

    In the less quality of calmer blood,

    To join the hands of two divided friends,   200

180–81.] *Dyce; in Q1–2 divided*
quarrel/ sir/ these/ climate.

---

186. *nick*] the point aimed at.

191–93. *hand . . . seal'd . . . delivery*] puns on the legal phrase "signed, sealed, and delivered."

194. *sticks*] possibly "clings" (to his property, Jane); this sense is not listed in *OED*.

199. *less quality*] apparently "blandness"; see the note on ll. 121–22.

Even these two that would offer willingly
Their own embrace.

AGER'S FRIEND.   Troth, she instructs you well,
Colonel, and you shall do a lover's part
Worth one brave act of valor.

COLONEL.   Why, I did
Misdoubt no scruple; is there doubt in it?   205

FITZALLEN.

Faith, sir, delays, which at the least are doubts.
But here's a constant resolution fix'd,
Which we wish willingly he would accord to.

COLONEL.

Tush, he shall do't; I will not be denied.
He owes me so much in the recompense   210
Of my reconcilement. Captain Ager,
You will take our parts against your uncle
In this quarrel?

CAPTAIN AGER.   I shall do my best, sir;
Two denials shall not repulse me. I love
Your worthy kinsman and wish him mine; I know   215
He doubts it not.

COLONEL.   See, he's returned.

Enter Russell *and a* Servant.

RUSSELL.   Your cue,
Be sure you keep it. 'Twill be spoken quickly;
Therefore watch it.   [*Exit* Servant.]

COLONEL.

Let's set on him all at once.

OMNES.   Sir, we have a suit to you.

RUSSELL.

What! All at once?

OMNES.   All, all, i'faith, sir.   220

RUSSELL.

One speaker may yet deliver. Say, say;
I shall not dare to stand out against so many.

COLONEL

'Faith, sir, here's a brabbling matter hangs on demur.

---

223. *brabbling*] disputing obstinately or noisily, wrangling.

I make the motion for all without a fee;
Pray you, let it be ended this term.

RUSSELL.   Ha, ha, ha!—   225
(*Aside.*) That's the rascal's cue, and he has miss'd it.—
What is it? What is it, sir?

COLONEL.   Why, sir, here's a man
And here's a woman. You're scholar good enough—
Put 'em together, and tell me what it spells.

RUSSELL.

Ha, ha, ha! —[*Aside.*] There's his cue once again.   230

                    Enter Servant.

Oh, he's come—humh!

SERVANT [*aside*].

My master laughs; that's his cue to mischief.

COLONEL.

What say you, sir?

SERVANT.   Sir.

RUSSELL.   Ha? what say you, sir?

SERVANT.

Sir, there's a couple desire speedily to speak with you.

RUSSELL.

A couple, sir, of what? Hounds or horses?   235

SERVANT.

Men, sir; gentlemen or yeomen, I know not which; but
the one sure they are.

RUSSELL.

Hast thou no other description of them?

SERVANT.

They come with commission, they say, sir, to taste of your
earth; if they like it, they'll turn it into gunpowder.   240

236–37.] *this edn.; in Q1–2 divided* which/ are.

───────────────────────────

223. *demur*] properly "demurrer"; in the law a request for dismissal
of a suit in Chancery because of a defect in the bill of complaint
(William West, *The Second Part of Symboleography*, 1611, sigs.
Cc3r–Cc3v).

RUSSELL.

Oh, they are saltpeter men, before me!
And they bring commission, the king's power indeed.
They must have entrance, but the knaves will be brib'd.
There's all the hope we have in officers;
They were too dangerous in a commonwealth,   245
But that they will be very well-corrupted—necessary varlets.

SERVANT.

Shall I enter in, sir?

RUSSELL.   By all fair means, sir,
And with all speed, sir; give 'em very good words,
To save my ground unravish'd, unbroke up.   [*Exit* Servant.]
Mine's yet a virgin earth; the worm hath not been seen   250
To wriggle in her chaste bowels; and I'd be loath
A gunpowder fellow should deflower her now.

COLONEL.

Our suit is yet delay'd by this means, sir.

RUSSELL.

Alas, I cannot help it! These fellows gone,
As I hope I shall dispatch 'em quickly,   255
A few articles shall conclude your suit.
Who? Master Fitzallen! The only man
That my adoption aims at.

COLONEL.   There's good hope, then.

Enter two Sergeants *in disguise.*

1 SERGEANT.

Save you, sir.

RUSSELL.

You are welcome, sir, for aught I know yet.   260

2 SERGEANT.

We come to take a view and taste of your ground, sir.

RUSSELL.

I had rather feed you with better meat, gentlemen;
But do your pleasures, pray.

---

241. *saltpeter men*] licensed searchers for nitrate with which to make gunpowder.

1 SERGEANT.   This is our pleasures—
    We arrest you, sir, in the King's name!

FITZALLEN.   Ha! At whose suit?

RUSSELL.
    How's that?

COLONEL.   Our weapons, good sir, furnish us!

JANE.   Ay me!   265

RUSSELL.
    Stay, stay, gentlemen, let's inquire the cause;
    It may be but a trifle, a small debt,
    Shall need no rescue here.

2 SERGEANT.
    Sir, betwixt three creditors, Master Leech, Master Swallow,
    and Master Bonesuck, the debts are a thousand pounds. 270

RUSSELL.
    A thousand pounds? Beshrew me, a good man's substance.

COLONEL.
    Good sir, our weapons! We'll teach these varlets to walk
    In their own particolor'd coats,
    That they may be distinguish'd from honest men.

263–64.] But . . . name] *this edn.;*   pounds/ substance.
in Q1–2 divided pray/ name.   272–74.] *this edn.; lines end* walk/
271.] *Dyce; in Q1–2 d i v i d e d*   they/ men *in Dyce; prose in Q1–2*

269–70. *three . . . pounds*] Since Russell has mentioned the debts earlier (l. 14), no doubt they are real and have been incurred as small, separate obligations; Fitzallen admits their existence by asking for bail (l. 289). But he denies knowing Leech, Swallow, and Bonesuck and consequently denies owing them money (ll. 310, 318). We are left in the dark with respect to how Russell arranged to fund Fitzallen's debts, making himself the sole creditor, but procuring, by using false names, a warrant for Fitzallen's arrest. Although Fitzallen suspects Russell's intervention (ll. 372–74), he is too puzzled to accuse him of false arrest. That Russell becomes sole creditor is shown by the speed with which he obtains Fitzallen's release a few days later (V.i.259–92.1).

271. *good man's*] In business parlance a *good man* was financially sound, able to meet all his commitments.

273. *particolor'd coats*] Apparently even lesser officials such as ushers and bailiffs, while on duty for a court, often wore gowns divided half and half into different colors, as did lawyers while pleading at the bar (George R. Corner, "Observations on Four Illuminations," *Archaelogia* 39 [1863]: 357–72).

1 SERGEANT.

    Sir, attempt no rescue; he's our prisoner.   275
    You'll make the danger worse by violence.

COLONEL.

    A plague upon your gunpowder treason!
    Ye quick damn'd varlets, is this your saltpeter proving,
    Your tasting earth? Would you might never feed better,
    Nor none of your catchpoll tribe!   280
    Our weapons, good sir, we'll yet deliver him.

RUSSELL.

    Pardon me, sir, I dare not suffer rescue here,
    At least not by so great an accessory
    As to furnish you; had you had your weapons—
    But to see the ill fate on't —[aside] my fine trick, i'faith. 285
    Let beggars beware to love rich men's daughters.
    I'll teach 'em the new morris; I learnt it
    Myself of another careful father.

FITZALLEN.

    May I not be bail'd?

2 SERGEANT.   Yes, but not with swords.

COLONEL.

    Slaves, here are sufficient men.

1 SERGEANT.   Aye, i'th' field,   290
    But not in the city, sir. If this gentleman
    Will be one, we'll easily admit the second.

RUSSELL.

    Who, I? Sir, pray, pardon me; I am wrong'd,
    Very much wrong'd in this; I must needs speak it.
    Sir, you have not dealt like an honest lover   295
    With me nor my child. Here you boast to me
    Of a great revenue, a large substance,

282.] *this edn.; in Q1–2 divided*
sir/ here.

---

280. *catchpoll*] a bailiff or sheriff's officer or sergeant, especially when
sent to arrest for debt.

290. *sufficient*] See the note on l. 271; a good man's sufficiency was
indicated by the presence of his name in the subsidy book (roll of
persons who paid real estate and other taxes levied by Parliament)
(William Lambard, *Eirenarcha*, 1602, sig. G1r).

Wherein you would endow and state my daughter.
Had I miss'd this, my opinion yet
Thought you a frugal man, to understand   300
The sure wards against all necessities;
Boldly to defend your wife and family;
To walk unmuffled, dreadless of these fleshhooks,
Even in the daring'st streets through all the city.
But now I find you a loose prodigal,   305
A large unthrift. A whole thousand pound?
Come from him, girl; his inside is not sound!

FITZALLEN.

Sir, I am wrong'd; these are malicious plots
Of some obscure enemies that I have;
These debts are none of mine.

RUSSELL.   Aye, all say so.   310
Perhaps you stand engag'd for other men;
If so you do, you must then call't your own;
The like arrearage do I run into
Should I bail you. But I have vow'd against it,
And I will keep my vows; that's religious.   315

FITZALLEN.

All this is nothing so, sir.

RUSSELL.   Nothing so?
By my faith, it is, sir; my vows are firm.

FITZALLEN.

I neither owe these debts nor engag'd for others.

RUSSELL.

The easier is your liberty regain'd;
These appear proofs to me.

COLONEL.   Liberty, sir?   320
I hope you'll not see him go to prison.

308.] *Dyce; in Q1–2 d i v i d e d*   318.] *this edn.; in Q1–2 divided*
wrong'd/ plots.   debts/ others.

---

298. *state*] cited by *OED* as the first instance of the sense "to
place, install in a dignity, office, right, etc."

314. *vow'd against it*] In a sermon published in 1602 William Burton
rebuked wealthy men who pretended to hold suretyship unlawful
and therefore took vows against it *(A Caveat for Suerties*, sigs. Ee5v–
Ee6r). Cf. Proverbs 11:15 and 22:26, 27.

RUSSELL.

    I do not mean to bear him company

    So far; but I'll see him out of my doors.

    Oh, sir, let him go to prison! 'Tis a school

    To tame wild bloods; he'll be much better for't.   325

COLONEL.

    Better for lying in prison!

RUSSELL.   In prison.

    Believe it, many an honest man lies in prison,

    Else all the keepers are knaves;

    They told me so themselves.

COLONEL.

    Sir, I do now suspect you have betray'd him,   330

    And us to cause us to be weaponless;

    If it be so, you're a blood-sucking churl,

    One that was born in a great frost, when charity

    Could not stir a finger; and you shall die

    In heat of a burning fever i'th' dog days,   335

    To begin your hell to you. I have said your grace for you;

    Now get you to supper as soon as you can;

    Pluto, the master of the house, is set already.

CAPTAIN AGER.

    Sir, you do wrong mine uncle.

COLONEL.   Pox on your uncle

    And all his kin, if my kinsman mingle no blood with 340

      him!

CAPTAIN AGER.

    You're a foul-mouth'd fellow.

COLONEL.   Foul-mouth'd I will be—

    Thou'rt the son of a whore.

CAPTAIN AGER.   Ha! Whore!

    Plagues and furies! I'll thrust that back

    Or pluck thy heart out after! Son of a whore!

340.] *this edn.; in Q1–2 divided*   341–43.] *this edn.; in Q1–2 divided*
mingle/ him.   fellow/ a whore/ back.

    333. *great frost*] like that of the winter of 1608, to which Rowley
also alludes in *A Search for Money* (1609), Percy Society Publications,
2 (London, 1840): iii. The Thames was then frozen hard from bank
to bank.

COLONEL.

On thy life I'll prove it.

CAPTAIN AGER.   Death, I am naked!   345

Uncle, I'll give you my left hand for my sword

To arm my right with. Oh, this fire will flame me

Into present ashes!

COLONEL.   Sir, give us weapons.

We ask our own; you will not rob us of them?

RUSSELL.

No, sir, but still restrain your furies here.   350

At my door I'll give you them, nor, at this time,

My nephew's; a time will better suit you.

And I must tell you, sir, you have spoke swords,

And 'gainst the law of arms poison'd the blades,

And with them wounded the reputation   355

Of an unblemish'd woman. Would you were out of my
doors!

COLONEL.

Pox on your doors, and let it run all your house o'er!

Give me my sword.

CAPTAIN AGER.   We shall meet, Colonel?

COLONEL.

Yes, better provided; to spur thee more,

I do repeat my words, "son of a whore."   360

Exit with his Friend.

AGER'S FRIEND.

Come, sir, 'tis no worse than 'twas;

You can do nothing now.

Exit Captain Ager *and his* Friend.

RUSSELL.

No, I'll bar him now. Away with that beggar!   *Exit.*

JANE.

Good sir, let this persuade you for two minutes' stay;

At this price, I know, you can wait all day. [*Gives money.*] 365

1 SERGEANT.

You know the remora that stays our ship always.

348. present] *Q2;* prsent *Q1.*

---

366. *remora*] or "echineis," a fish having a vacuum-making organ
on its head by means of which it attaches itself to other fish and

JANE.

    Your ship sinks many when this hold lets go.
    Oh, my Fitzallen, what is to be done?

FITZALLEN.

    To be still thine is all my part to be,
    Whether in freedom or captivity.   370

JANE.

    But art thou so engag'd as this pretends?

FITZALLEN.

    By heaven, sweet Jane, 'tis all a hellish plot!
    Your cruel smiling father all this while
    Has candied o'er a bitter pill for me,
    Thinking by my remove to plant some other,   375
    And then let go his fangs.

JANE.   Plant some other?
    Thou hast too firmly stamp'd me for thine own
    Ever to be ras'd out; I am not current
    In any other's hand; I fear too soon
    I shall discover it.

FITZALLEN.   Let come the worst;   380
    Bind but this knot with an unloosed line,
    I will be still thine own.

JANE.   And I'll be thine.

1 SERGEANT.

    My watch has gone two minutes, master.

FITZALLEN.

    It shall not be renew'd; I go, sir. Farewell!

JANE.

    Farewell! we both are prison'd, though not together.   385
    But here's the difference in our luckless chance:
    I fear mine own, wish thy deliverance.

FITZALLEN.

    Our hearts shall hourly visit; I'll send to thee.

---

turtles (without harm to the host) and sometimes adheres to boats.
Pliny says the remora "is believed to make ships go more slowly by
sticking to their hulls," but he does not say he has observed the
fact (*Natural History*, vol. 3, trans. H. Rackham [Cambridge, Mass.,
1940], Book 9, chap. 41). *Remora* means "delay."

Then 'tis no prison where the mind is free.

Exit Fitzallen *with* Sergeants.

Enter Russell.

RUSSELL.

So, let him go. Now, wench, I bring thee joys,   390
A fair sunshine after this angry storm.
It was my policy to remove this beggar;
What! Shall rich men wed their only daughters
To two fair suits of clothes? And perhaps yet
The poor tailor is unpaid. No, no, my girl,   395
I have a lad of thousands coming in.
Suppose he have more wealth than wit to guide it;
Why, there's thy gains; thou keep'st the keys of all,
Disposest all. And for generation,
Man does most seldom stamp 'em from the brain;   400
Wise men beget fools, and fools are the fathers
To many wise children. Hysteron proteron,
A great scholar may beget an idiot,
And from the plow tail may come a great scholar;
Nay, they are frequent propagations.   405

JANE.

I am not well, sir.

RUSSELL.   Ha? Not well, my girl?
Thou shalt have a physician then,
The best that gold can fetch upon his footcloth.
Thou knowest my tender pity to thee ever;
Want nothing that thy wishes can instruct thee   410
To call for; 'fore me, and thou look'st half ill indeed.
But I'll bring one within a day to thee
Shall rouse thee up; for he's come up already,
One Master Chough, a Cornish gentleman.
'Has as much land of his own fee-simple   415
As a crow can fly over in half a day;

---

402. *Hysteron proteron*] a figure of speech in which a word or phrase that should properly come last is put first; but *OED* cites this instance for the sense "inversion of the natural order of things."

408. *footcloth*] an ornamented cloth laid over a horse's back and hanging to the ground on either side; a mark of dignity.

And now I think on't, at the Crow at Aldgate
His lodging is. He shall so stir thee up!
Come, come, be cheer'd; think of thy preferment,
Honor, and attendance; these will bring thee health,   420
And the way to 'em is to climb by wealth.   *Exeunt.*

[II.i]   *Enter* Captain Ager.

CAPTAIN AGER.
The son of a whore?
There is not such another murdering piece
In all the stock of calumny; it kills
At one report two reputations,
A mother's and a son's. If it were possible   5
That souls could fight after the bodies fell,
This were a quarrel for 'em. He should be one indeed
That never heard of heaven's joys or hell's torments
To fight this out; I am too full of conscience,
Knowledge and patience, to give justice to't;   10
So careful of my eternity, which consists
Of upright actions, that unless I knew
It were a truth I stood for, any coward
Might make my breast his footpace. And who lives
That can assure the truth of his conception,   15
More than a mother's carriage makes it hopeful?
And is't not miserable valor then
That man should hazard all upon things doubtful?

---

5. *mother's . . . son's*] One "deprived of naturall honor, is incapable of any other . . ."; a mother's unchastity deprives her children of native honor, without which perfect honor cannot be acquired (Sir John Kepers, *The Courtiers Academie*, 1598, sigs. P3r–P3v).

11. *careful . . . eternity*] As Sampson notes, p. 393, Ager's need to have reassurance of his mother's purity becomes a credible motive in the light of Elizabethan acceptance of the duel as a trial by combat. In this trial the man who defends a lie provokes the wrath of God (and consequently his own defeat) and may suffer death and damnation. A prudent man will not thus *hazard all upon things doubtful* (l. 18). See my Introduction, above, p. xxiii.

14. *footpace*] a carpet, a mat, or a step in a staircase.

15. *assure . . . conception*] be certain of his legitimacy.

Oh, there's the cruelty of my foe's advantage!
Could but my soul resolve my cause were just,   20
Earth's mountain, nor sea's surge should hide him from me;
E'en to hell's threshold would I follow him
And see the slanderer in before I left him!
But as it is, it fears me; and I never
Appear'd too conscionably just till now.   25
My good opinion of her life and virtues
Bids me go on, and fain would I be rul'd by't;
But when my judgment tells me she's but woman,
Whose frailty let in death to all mankind,
My valor shrinks at that. Certain she's good;   30
There only wants but my assurance in't,
And all things then were perfect. How I thirst for't!
Here comes the only she that could resolve,
But 'tis too vild a question to demand indeed.

Enter the Lady Ager.

LADY AGER.
    Son, I've a suit to you.
CAPTAIN AGER [*aside*].   That may do well.—   35
    To me, good madam? You're most sure to speed in't,
    Be't i'my power to grant it.
LADY AGER.   'Tis my love
    Makes the request, that you would never part
    From England more.
CAPTAIN AGER.   With all my heart 'tis granted;
    I'm sure I'm i'th' way never to part from't.   40
LADY AGER.
    Where left you your dear friend the Colonel?
CAPTAIN AGER.
    Oh, the dear Colonel—I should meet him soon.

29. Frailty] *Dyce*; fraileto *Q1*
fraeltie to *Q2*.

34. *vild*] equivalent to "vile" in its adjectival senses. *Vild* is a very
common form in the early seventeenth century.

LADY AGER.

    Oh, fail him not then. He's a gentleman
    The fame and reputation of your time
    Is much engag'd to.

CAPTAIN AGER.   Yes, and you knew all, mother.   45

LADY AGER.

    I thought I'd known so much of his fair goodness
    More could not have been look'd for.

CAPTAIN AGER.   Oh, yes, yes, madam.
    And this his last exceeded all the rest.

LADY AGER.

    For gratitude's sake let me know this, I prithee.

CAPTAIN AGER.

    Then thus—and I desire your censure freely,   50
    Whether it appear'd not a strange noble kindness in him.

LADY AGER.

    Trust me, I long to hear't.

CAPTAIN AGER.   You know he's hasty—
    That by the way.

LADY AGER.   So are the best conditions;
    Your father was the like.

CAPTAIN AGER [aside].   I begin now
    To doubt me more; why am not I so too then?   55
    Blood follows blood through forty generations,
    And I've a slow pac'd wrath—a shrewd dilemma!—

LADY AGER.

    Well, as you were saying, sir.

CAPTAIN AGER.   Marry, thus, good madam:
    There was in company a foul-mouth'd villain; stay, stay—
    Who should I liken him to, that you have seen?   60
    He comes so near one that I would not match him with;
    Faith, just o'th' Colonel's pitch. He's ne'er the worse man;
    Usurers have been compar'd to magistrates,
    Extortioners to lawyers, and the like,
    But they all prove ne'er the worse men for that.   65

64. Extortioners] *Q2*; Extortiners
Q1.

---

53. *conditions*] disposition or cast of mind.

LADY AGER.

That's bad enough; they need not.

CAPTAIN AGER.   This rude fellow,

A shame to all humanity or manners,

Breathes from the rottenness of his gall and malice

The foulest stain that ever man's fame blemish'd,

Part of which fell upon your honor, madam,   70

Which heighten'd my affliction.

LADY AGER.   Mine? My honor, sir?

CAPTAIN AGER.

The Colonel soon enrag'd, as he's all touchwood,

Takes fire before me, makes the quarrel his,

Appoints the field; my wrath could not be heard

His was so high pitch'd, so gloriously mounted.   75

Now, what's the friendly fear that fights within me,

Should his brave, noble fury undertake

A cause that were unjust in our defense,

And so to lose him everlastingly

In that dark depth where all bad quarrels sink   80

Never to rise again! What pity 'twere

First to die here and never to die there!

LADY AGER.

Why, what's the quarrel—speak, sir—that should raise

Such fearful doubt, my honor bearing part on't?

The words, whate'er they were?

CAPTAIN AGER.   Son of a whore.   85

LADY AGER.

Thou liest!   *Strikes him.*

And were my love ten thousand times more to thee,

Which is as much now as e'er mother's was,

So thou shouldst feel my anger. Dost thou call

That quarrel doubtful? Where are all my merits?   90

Not one stand up to tell this man his error?

72.] *Dyce; in Q1–2 divided* en-   86–87.] *Dyce; one line in Q1–2,*
rag'd/ touchwood.   *where S.D. follows l. 90.*
84. Such] *Q1 (corr.);* Snch *(un-*
corr.).

---

62. *pitch*] summit, height.

Thou might'st as well bring the sun's truth in question
As thy birth or my honor.

CAPTAIN AGER.   Now blessings crown you for't!
It is the joyful'st blow that e'er flesh felt.

LADY AGER.

Nay, stay, stay, sir, thou art not left so soon;   95
This is no question to be slighted off,
And at your pleasure clos'd up fair again
As though you'd never touch'd it. No, honor doubted
Is honor deeply wounded; and it rages
More than a common smart, being of thy making.   100
For thee to fear my truth, it kills my comfort.
Where should fame seek for her reward, when he
That is her own by the great tie of blood
Is farthest off in bounty? Oh, poor goodness!
That only pay'st thy self with thy own works,   105
For nothing else looks towards thee. Tell me, pray,
Which of my loving cares dost thou requite
With this vild thought? Which of my prayers or wishes?
Many thou owest me for; this seven year hast thou known
    me
A widow, only married to my vow;   110
That's no small witness of my faith and love
To him that in life was thy honor'd father.
And live I now to know that good mistrusted?

CAPTAIN AGER.

No, 't shall appear that my belief is cheerful,
For never was a mother's reputation   115
Noblier defended. 'Tis my joy and pride
I have a firm faith to bestow upon it.

LADY AGER.

What's that you said, sir?

CAPTAIN AGER.   'Twere too bold and soon yet
To crave forgiveness of you. I will earn it first;
Dead or alive, I know I shall enjoy it.   120

117. faith] *Dyce; not in Q1–2.*

---

120. *dead or alive*] Although Ager is now convinced he will con-
quer the Colonel and vindicate her honor, he himself might still
suffer a fatal wound.

LADY AGER.

What's all this, sir?

CAPTAIN AGER.   My joy's beyond expression!

I do but think how wretched I had been

Were this another's quarrel, and not mine.

LADY AGER.

Why, is it yours?

CAPTAIN AGER.   Mine! Think me not so miserable,

Not to be mine! Then were I worse than abject,   125

More to be loath'd than vileness or sin's dunghill;

Nor did I fear your goodness, faithful madam,

But came with greedy joy to be confirm'd in't,

To give the nobler onset. Then shines valor,

And admiration from her fix'd sphere draws,   130

When it comes burnish'd with a righteous cause;

Without which I'm ten fathoms under coward

That now am ten degrees above a man,

Which is but one of virtue's easiest wonders.

LADY AGER.

But, pray, stay; all this while I understood you   135

The Colonel was the man.

CAPTAIN AGER.   Yes, he's the man,

The man of injury, reproach, and slander,

Which I must turn into his soul again.

LADY AGER.

The Colonel do't? That's strange.

CAPTAIN AGER.   The villain did it;

That's not so strange—your blessing and your leave.   140

LADY AGER.

Come, come, you shall not go.

CAPTAIN AGER.   Not go! Were death

Sent now to summon me to my eternity,

I'd put him off an hour. Why, the whole world

Has not chains strong enough to bind me from't;

The strongest is my reverence to you,   145

Which if you force upon me in this case,

I must be forc'd to break it.

LADY AGER.   Stay, I say!

— 31 —

CAPTAIN AGER.

 In any thing command me but in this, madam.

LADY AGER [*aside*].

 'Las, I shall lose him! —You'll hear me first!

CAPTAIN AGER.

 At my return I will.

LADY AGER.   You'll never hear me more, then.   150

CAPTAIN AGER.

 How?

LADY AGER.   Come back, I say!

 You may well think there's cause I call so often.

CAPTAIN AGER.

 Hah, cause! What cause?

LADY AGER.   So much, you must not go.

CAPTAIN AGER.

 How?

LADY AGER.   You must not go.

CAPTAIN AGER.

 Must not! Why?

LADY AGER.   I know a reason for't   155

 Which I could wish you'd yield to, and not know.

 If not, it must come forth. Faith, do not know,

 And yet obey my will.

CAPTAIN AGER.   Why, I desire

 To know no other than the cause I have,

 Nor should you wish it, if you take your injury;   160

 For one more great, I know the world includes not.

LADY AGER.

 Yes, one that makes this nothing—yet be rul'd,

 And if you understand not, seek no further.

CAPTAIN AGER.

 I must, for this is nothing.

LADY AGER.   Then take all;

 And if amongst it you receive that secret   165

 That will offend you, though you condemn me,

 Yet blame yourself a little, for perhaps

 I would have made my reputation sound

160. injury;] *Sampson;* iniury *Q1–
2.*

Upon another's hazard with less pity;
But upon yours I dare not.

CAPTAIN AGER.   How?

LADY AGER.   I dare not;   170
'Twas your own seeking, this.

CAPTAIN AGER.   If you mean evilly,
I cannot understand you; nor for all the riches
This life has, would I.

LADY AGER.   Would you never might!

CAPTAIN AGER.
Why, your goodness, that I joy to fight for.

LADY AGER.
In that you neither right your joy nor me.   175

CAPTAIN AGER.
What an ill orator has virtue got here!
Why, shall I dare to think it a thing possible
That you were ever false?

LADY AGER.   Oh, fearfully!
As much as you come to.

CAPTAIN AGER.   O silence, cover me!
I've felt a deadlier wound than man can give me. 180
False?

LADY AGER.   I was betray'd to a most sinful hour
By a corrupted soul I put in trust once,
A kinswoman.

CAPTAIN AGER.   Where is she? Let me pay her.

LADY AGER.
Oh, dead long since.

CAPTAIN AGER.   Nay, then, sh'as all her wages.
False! Do not say't, for honor's goodness do not! 185
You never could be so. He I call'd father
Deserv'd you at your best, when youth and merit
Could boast at highest in you; y'ad no grace
Or virtue that he match'd not, no delight
That you invented but he sent it crown'd   190
To your full wishing soul.

LADY AGER.   That heaps my guiltiness.

180–81.] *Dyce; in Q1–2 divided*
me, false/ hour.

CAPTAIN AGER.

    Oh, were you so unhappy to be false
    Both to your self and me, but to me chiefly?
    What a day's hope is here lost, and with it
    The joys of a just cause! Had you but thought   195
    On such a noble quarrel, you'd ha' died
    Ere you'd ha' yielded, for the sin's hate first,
    Next for the shame of this hour's cowardice.
    Curst be the heat that lost me such a cause,
    A work that I was made for. Quench, my spirit,   200
    And out with honor's flaming lights within thee!
    Be dark and dead to all respects of manhood;
    I never shall have use of valor more.
    Put off your vow for shame! Why should you hoard up
    Such justice for a barren widowhood,   205
    That was so injurious to the faith of wedlock?   *Exit* Lady.
    I should be dead, for all my life's work's ended.
    I dare not fight a stroke now, nor engage
    The noble resolution of my friends;

        Enter two Friends *of Captain Ager's.*

    That were more vild. They're here. Kill me, my shame!   210
    I am not for the fellowship of honor.
1 AGER'S FRIEND.

    Captain, fie! Come, sir, we have been seeking for you
    Very late today; this was not wont to be.
    Your enemy's i'th' field.
CAPTAIN AGER.   Truth enters cheerfully.
2 AGER'S FRIEND.

    Good faith, sir, y'ave a royal quarrel on't.   215
CAPTAIN AGER.

    Yes, in some other country, Spain or Italy,
    It would be held so.
1 AGER'S FRIEND.   How? And is't not here so?
CAPTAIN AGER.

    'Tis not so contumeliously receiv'd
    In these parts, and you mark it.

206. wedlock] *Q1 (corr.);* wedlorke
Q1 (uncorr.).

---

1 AGER'S FRIEND.   Not in these?
    Why, prithee, what is more, or can be?
CAPTAIN AGER.   Yes,   220
    That ordinary commotioner, the lie,
    Is father of most quarrels in this climate,
    And held here capital, and you go to that.
2 AGER'S FRIEND.
    But, sir, I hope you will not go to that,
    Or change your own for it. "Son of a whore!"   225
    Why, there's the lie down to posterity,
    The lie to birth, the lie to honesty.
    Why would you cozen yourself so and beguile
    So brave a cause, manhood's best masterpiece?
    Do you ever hope for one so brave again?   230
CAPTAIN AGER.
    Consider, then, the man, the Colonel,
    Exactly worthy, absolutely noble,
    However spleen and rage abuses him;
    And 'tis not well nor manly to pursue
    A man's infirmity.
1 AGER'S FRIEND.   Oh, miracle!   235
    So hopeful, valiant, and complete a captain
    Possess'd with a tame devil! Come out! Thou spoilest
    The most improv'd young soldier of seven kingdoms,
    Made captain at nineteen, which was deserv'd
    The year before, but honor comes behind still!   240
    Come out, I say, this was not wont to be;
    That spirit never stood in need of provocation,
    Nor shall it now. Away, sir!
CAPTAIN AGER.   Urge me not.
1 AGER'S FRIEND.
    By manhood's reverend honor but we must.
CAPTAIN AGER.
    I will not fight a stroke.
1 AGER'S FRIEND.   Oh, blasphemy   245
    To sacred valor!
CAPTAIN AGER.   Lead me where you list.

227. birth] *Dyce;* brithe *Q1–2.*   231. man, the Colonel] *Dyce;* man
                                        Colonel *Q1–2.*

1 AGER'S FRIEND.

    Pardon this traitorous slumber, clog'd with evils.
    Give captains rather wives than such tame devils.   *Exeunt.*

[II.ii]   *Enter* Physician *and* Jane.

PHYSICIAN.

    Nay, mistress, you must not be cover'd to me;
    The patient must ope to the physician
    All her dearest sorrows. Art is blinded else
    And cannot show her mystical effects.

JANE.

    Can art be so dim-sighted, learned sir?   5
    I did not think her so incapacious.
    You train me, as I guess, like a conjuror,
    One of our five oraculous wizards,
    Who, from the help of his examinant,
    By the near guess of his suspicion   10
    Appoints out the thief by the marks he tells him.
    Have you no skill in physiognomy?
    What color, says your coat, is my disease?
    I am unmarried, and it cannot be yellow;

1. mistress] *Dyce;* Master *Q1–2.*

---

    1. *cover'd*] "secretive," apparently; in *OED* the sense "secret" is not cited after 1581.

    3. *dearest*] most dangerous.

    3. *sorrows*] injuries; the sense "physical pain" is not cited in *OED* for after the year 1398. But no doubt *dangerous sorrows* also means "bitterest griefs."

    4. *mystical*] secret, unavowed.

    6. *incapacious*] unable to comprehend or apprehend (this instance is cited in *OED*).

    7. *train*] entice.

    8. *five*] Dyce and later editors emend to "fine"; but possibly *five* had a topical meaning now obscure.

    12. *physiognomy*] The judging of character by the shape and color of the features had been a doubtful science for many centuries (Carroll Camden, "The Mind's Construction in the Face," *Philological Quarterly* 20 [1941]: 400–12).

    14. *yellow*] color of jealousy in married persons.

If it be maiden green, you cannot miss it.   15
PHYSICIAN.
    I cannot see that vacuum in your blood.
    But, gentlewoman, if you love your self,
    Love my advice; be free and plain with me.
    Where lies your grief?
JANE.   Where lies my grief indeed?
    I cannot tell the truth where my grief lies,   20
    But my joy's imprison'd.
PHYSICIAN.   This is mystical.
JANE.
    Lord, what plain questions you make problems of!
    Your art is such a regular highway
    That put you out of it, and you are lost.
    My heart is imprison'd in my body, sir;   25
    There's all my joy, and my sorrow too
    Lies very near it.
PHYSICIAN..   They are bad adjuncts.
    Your joy and grief, lying so near together,
    Can propagate no happy issue; remove
    The one (and let it be the worst), your grief,   30
    If you'll propose the best unto your joy.
JANE.
    Why, now comes your skill. What physic for it?
PHYSICIAN.
    Now I have found you out; you are in love.
JANE.
    I think I am. What your appliance now?
    Can all your Paracelsian mixtures cure it?   35
    'T must be a surgeon of the civil law,
    I fear, that must cure me.

---

15. *maiden green*] greensickness, or chlorosis, an anemia of young
women; at that time thought to be curable by marriage.

16. *vacuum*] thinness (Sampson); *OED* cites this instance of the
term as figurative, but does not state the sense.

35. *Paracelsian*] Metrical, not medical, reasons probably led Rowley
to use this term instead of *Galenical*. Paracelsus, by advocating experiment and the use of chemicals as remedies, created a party opposed to
the Galenists.

36. *surgeon . . . law*] a clergyman. Because canon and civil law both
originated in Roman law, divines studied both at the universities.

PHYSICIAN.   Gentlewoman,
 If you knew well my heart, you would not be
 So circular; the very common name
 Of physician might reprove your niceness.   40
 We are as secret as your confessors,
 And as firm oblig'd; 'tis a fine like death
 For us to blab.
JANE.   I will trust you. Yet, sir,
 I had rather do it by attorney to you;
 I else have blushes that will stop my tongue. 45
 Have you no friend so friendly as yourself,
 Of mine own sex, to whom I might impart
 My sorrows to you at the second hand?
PHYSICIAN.
 Why, law, there I hit you; and be confirm'd,
 I'll give you such a bosom counselor   50
 That your own tongue shall be sooner false to you.
 Make yourself unready, and be naked to her;
 I'll fetch her presently.   *Exit* Physician.
JANE.   I must reveal;
 My shame will else take tongue, and speak before me.
 'Tis a necessity impulsive drives me.   55
 Oh my hard fate! But my more hard father,
 That father of my fate! A father, said I?
 What a strange paradox I run into!
 I must accuse two fathers of my fate
 And fault, a reciprocal generation;   60
 The father of my fault would have repair'd
 His faulty issue, but my fate's father hinders it.
 Then fate and fault, wherever I begin,
 I must blame both; and yet 'twas love did sin.

    Enter Physician, *and* Anne *his sister.*

PHYSICIAN.
 Look you, mistress, here's your closet; put in 65
 What you please; you ever keep the key of it.

---

40. *niceness*] reserve, shyness.
52. *Make yourself unready*] undress.

JANE.
  Let me speak private, sir.
PHYSICIAN.   With all my heart.
  I will be more than mine ear's length from you.   [*Retires.*]
JANE.
  You hold some endeared place with this gentleman.
ANNE.
  He's my brother, forsooth, I his creature;   70
  He does command me any lawful office
  Either in act or counsel.
JANE.   I must not doubt you;
  Your brother has protested secrecy,
  And strengthen'd me in you, I must lay ope
  A guilty sorrow to you: I am with child.   75
  'Tis no black swan I show you; these spots stick
  Upon the face of many go for maids.
  I that had face enough to do the deed
  Cannot want tongue to speak it; but 'tis to you,
  Whom I accept my helper.
ANNE.   Mistress, 'tis lock'd   80
  Within a castle that's invincible;
  It is too late to wish it were undone.
JANE.
  I have scarce a wish within myself so strong;
  For, understand me, 'tis not all so ill
  As you may yet conceit it; this deed was done   85
  When heaven had witness to the jugal knot.

---

72. *doubt*] suspect (of falsehood).

76. *black swan*] rare thing; from Juvenal *Sat.* 6. 165: *Rara avis in terris nigroque simillima cycno* (with reference to the scarcity of chaste women).

86. heaven . . . knot] There was a precontract properly witnessed by two lay persons; and since intercourse has followed, the marriage is valid, even if it was made only *per verba de futuro*. But the couple are liable to ecclesiastical punishment because of omitting the Church's blessing and the use of a priest as witness. (Though the witnesses are never identified, there is no need to doubt the couple's assertions; cf. V.i.363–69.) (Gibson, 1: 416–17; Frederick Pollock and F. M. Maitland, *The History of English Law Before the Time of Edward I*, 2nd ed. [Cambridge, 1923], 2: 368–69.)

Only the barren ceremony wants,
Which by an adverse father is abridged.

ANNE.

Would my pity could help you!

JANE.   Your counsel may.

My father yet shoots widest from my sorrow   90
And with a care indulgent, seeing me chang'd
From what I was, sends for your good brother
To find my grief and practice remedy.
You know it; give it him; but if a fourth
Be added to this counsel, I will say   95
Ye're worse than you can call me at the worst,
At this advantage of my reputation.

ANNE.

I will revive a reputation
That women long has lost; I'll keep counsel.
I'll only now oblige my teeth to you,   100
And they shall bite the blabber if it offer
To breath on an offending syllable.

JANE.

I trust you; go, whisper. Here comes my father.

Enter Russell, Chough, *and* Trimtram.

RUSSELL.

Sir, you are welcome, more, and most welcome,
All the degrees of welcome; thrice welcome, sir.   105

CHOUGH.

Is this your daughter, sir?

---

103. *whisper*] "whisper this information to your brother."

103.1. *Chough*] The word *chuff* had several senses appropriate to this person: (1) a chatterer, a jackdaw; (2) a boor; (3) an avaricious man (avarice is implicit in Chough's plan for marriage). Cf. John Marston's line in *The Scourge of Villanie* (Bodley Head Quarto, ed. G. B. Harrison [London, 1925], p. 48): ". . . Tricksey tales of speaking Cornish dawes."

103.1. *Trimtram*] Besides the proverb "Trim, tram, like master, like man," in the sixteenth century, this word suggested a piece of absurdity or nonsense (*OED*) and, above all, apishness. A juggler called his monkey thus: "Sir Tristram Trimtram, come aloft, Jackanapes, with a whim-wham" (Marston, *The Malcontent*, ed. M. L. Wine, [Lincoln, Nebr., 1964], I.iii.55–56).

RUSSELL.   Mine only joy, sir.

CHOUGH.

I'll show her the Cornish hug, sir— I have kiss'd you now,
sweetheart, and I never do any kindness to my friends,
but I use to hit 'em in the teeth with it presently

TRIMTRAM.

My name is Trimtram, forsooth; look what my master   110
does, I use to do the like.   [*Offers to kiss* Anne.]

ANNE.

You are deceiv'd, sir; I am not this gentlewoman's servant, to make your courtesy equal.

CHOUGH.

You do not know me, mistress.

JANE.

No indeed—[*aside*] I doubt I shall learn too soon.   115

CHOUGH.

My name is Chough, a Cornish gentleman. My man's
mine own countryman too, i'faith; I warrant you took us
for some of the small islanders.

JANE.

I did indeed, between the Scotch and Irish.

CHOUGH.

Red-shanks? I thought so, by my truth. No, truly, we are 120
right Cornish diamonds.

TRIMTRAM.

Yes, we cut out quarrels and break glasses where we go.

---

107. *Cornish hug*] a formidable hold, "the fruit whereof is [a] fair
fall or foil at the least" (John Ray, *A Compleat Collection of English
Proverbs* [London, 1768], p. 237).

109. *hit . . . teeth*] "to reproach with," upbraid, censure (Tilley, T
429). Chough jokes that, having favored Jane with a specimen of
a hug, he upbraids her ingratitude with a kiss.

110. *look what*] whatever.

115. *doubt*] fear.

120. *Red-shanks*] vulgar term for the Scottish and Irish peasantry
(Jane seems to refer to the Hebrideans or Manx, l. 119). The Cornish
crow, called also a *chuff*, has a red bill and red legs. Probably Chough
and Trimtram wore red stockings.

121. *Cornish diamonds*] quartz crystals of a kind peculiar to
Cornwall.

122. *quarrels*] diamond-shaped panes of glass.

PHYSICIAN [*to* Anne].

> If it be hidden from her father, yet
> His ignorance understands well his knowledge;
> For this I guess to be some rich coxcomb   125
> He'd put upon his daughter.

ANNE.   That's plainly so.

PHYSICIAN.

> Then only she's beholding to our help
> For the close delivery of her burden,
> Else all's overthrown.

ANNE.   And pray be faithful in that, sir.

PHYSICIAN.

> Tush, we physicians are the truest   130
> Alchemists, that from the ore and dross of sin
> Can new distil a maidenhead again.

RUSSELL.

> How do you like her, sir?

CHOUGH.

> Troth, I do like her, sir, in the way of comparison, to any
> thing that a man would desire. I am as high as the Mount 135
> in love with her already, and that's as far as I can go by
> land, but I hope to go further by water with her one day.

RUSSELL.

> I tell you, sir, she has lost some color
> By wrestling with a peevish sickness now of late.

CHOUGH.

> Wrestle? Nay, and she love wrestling, I'll teach her a trick 140
> to overthrow any peevish sickness in London, whate'er
> it be.

RUSSELL.

> Well, she had a rich beauty though I say't;
> Nor is it lost; a little thing repairs it.

127. our] *Q2;* out *Q1.*

---

124. *His . . . knowledge*] "His ignorance of his daughter's pregnancy causes his mercenary device of marrying her off at once to
seem like a feat of worldly wisdom."

128. *close*] secret.

135. *Mount*] St. Michael's Mount, just east of Penzance.

139. *peevish*] malignant, harmful.

CHOUGH.

    She shall command the best thing that I have in Middle- 145
    sex, i'faith.

RUSSELL.

    Well, sir, talk with her; give her a relish
    Of your good liking to her. You shall have time
    And free access to finish what you now begin.
                              [Russell *talks to* Physician.]

JANE [*aside*].

    What means my father? My love's unjust restraint,   150
    My shame were it publish'd, both together
    Could not afflict me like this odious fool.
    Now I see why he hated my Fitzallen.

CHOUGH.

    Sweet lady, your father says you are a wrestler; if you love
    that sport, I love you the better. I'faith, I love it as well 155
    as I love my meat after supper; 'tis indeed meat, drink,
    and cloth to me.

JANE.

    Methinks it should tear your clothes, sir.

CHOUGH.

    Not a rag, i'faith. Trimtram, hold my cloak. —I'll wrestle
    a fall with you now; I'll show you a trick that you never 160
    saw in your life.

JANE.

    Oh, good sir, forbear! I am no wrestler.

PHYSICIAN.

    Good sir, take heed, you'll hurt the gentlewoman.

CHOUGH.

    I will not catch beneath the waist, believe it; I know fair
    play.   165

JANE.

    'Tis no woman's exercise in London, sir.

CHOUGH.

    I'll ne'er believe that. The hug and the lock between man

145–46. Middlesex, i'faith.] *Dyce;*
yfaith, [*at left margin*] Middlesex.
[*at right margin*] *Q1–2.*

167. *lock*] grip or grapple.

and woman, with a fair fall, is as sweet an exercise for
the body as you'll desire in a summer's evening.

PHYSICIAN.

Sir, the gentlewoman is not well.   170

CHOUGH.

It may be you are a physician, sir.

PHYSICIAN.

'Tis so, sir.

CHOUGH.

I say, then, and I'll stand to't, three ounces of wrestling
with two hips, a yard of a green gown put together in the
inturn, is as good a medicine for the green sickness as 175
ever breath'd.

TRIMTRAM.

Come, sir, take your cloak again; I see here will be ne'er
a match.

JANE [aside].

A match? I'd rather be match'd from a musket's mouth
and shot unto my death.   180

CHOUGH.

I'll wrestle with any man for a good supper.

TRIMTRAM.

Aye, marry, sir, I'll take your part there, catch that catch
may.

PHYSICIAN.

Sir, she is willing to't. There at my house
She shall be private, and near to my attendance.   185
I know you not mistrust my faithful care;
I shall return her soon and perfectly.

RUSSELL.

Take your charge, sir. Go with this gentleman, Jane.
But, prithee, look well this way ere thou go'st;

---

174. *green*] "grass-stained" (Sampson); *green gown* was a common
euphemism for loss of virginity.

175. *inturn*] in wrestling the putting of a leg between the opponent's thighs and lifting him up.

182–83. *catch . . . may*] to lay hold of, each as he can (*OED* gives
the sense of a particular kind of wrestling only for the nineteenth
century).

'Tis a rich simplicity of great estate,   190
A thing that will be rul'd, and thou shalt rule.
Consider of your sex's general aim,
That domination is a woman's heaven.

JANE.

I'll think on't, sir.

RUSSELL.   My daughter is retiring, sir.

CHOUGH.

I will part at Dartmouth with her, sir. [*Kisses her.*] Oh, 195
that thou didst but love wrestling! I would give any man
three foils on that condition.

TRIMTRAM.

There's three sorts of men that would thank you for 'em,
either cutlers, fencers, or players.

RUSSELL.

Sir, as I began, I end—wondrous welcome!   200

Exit Russell, Jane, Physician, Anne.

TRIMTRAM.

What, will you go to school today? You are enter'd, you
know, and your quarterage runs on.

CHOUGH.

What? To the roaring school? Pox on't, 'tis such a dam-
nable noise, I shall never attain it, neither. I do wonder
they have never a wrestling school; that were worth 205
twenty of your fencing or dancing schools.

TRIMTRAM.

Well, you must learn to roar here in London; you'll
never proceed in the reputation of gallantry else.

CHOUGH.

How long has roaring been an exercise, thinkest thou,
Trimtram?   210

---

197. *foils*] A foil is a throw that is not a flat fall; an almost-fall.
In some cases, two foils made a fall. Chough means a handicap.

202. *quarterage*] quarterly charges.

203. *roaring school*] Roarers, or roaring boys, were professional
bullies, drunken and lecherous. See Appendix B, "The Roaring
School," below.

TRIMTRAM.

Ever since guns came up; the first was your Roaring Meg.

CHOUGH.

Meg? Then 'twas a woman was the first roarer.

TRIMTRAM.

Aye, afire of her touch-hole, that cost many a proper
man's life since that time; and then the lions, they learnt
it from the guns, living so near 'em; then it was heard 215
to the Bankside, and the bears they began to roar; then
the boys got it, and so ever since there have been a company of roaring boys.

CHOUGH.

And how long will it last, thinkest thou?

TRIMTRAM.

As long as the water runs under London Bridge, or wa- 220
termen at Westminster stairs.

CHOUGH.

Well, I will begin to roar too, since it is in fashion. O
Corineus, this was not in thy time! I should have heard
on't by the tradition of mine ancestors—for I'm sure there
were Choughs in thy days—if it had been so; when Her- 225
cules and thou wert on the Olympic mount together,
then was wrestling in request.

---

211. *Roaring Meg*] any huge piece of ordnance *(OED)*; so called
after a very large cannon in Edinburgh Castle; a similar piece in the
Tower was called Long Meg (Sampson).

214–15. *lions . . . 'em*] Lions were kept in the Tower.

216. *Bankside . . . bears*] Bears were kept for baiting at Paris
Garden and the Hope Theater in Southwark (the Bankside), across
the Thames southwesterly from the Tower.

220. *water . . . Bridge*] The roaring of the tide around the piers
of the Bridge is often mentioned by Elizabethans.

220–21. *watermen at Westminster*] Having rowed the long trip to
their western terminus, the hired wherrymen did not wish to return
to the City without a fare. Thomas Dekker compares them to "whole
kennels of yelping" dogs, in *A Knights Coniuring*, 1607, sig. F1r.

223. *Corineus*] companion of Brut and founder of Cornwall, wrestler
with the giant Gogmagog at Plymouth. For one account see Michael
Drayton, *Poly-Olbion*, Song 1, ll. 471–506.

TRIMTRAM.

    Aye, and that mount is now the Mount in Cornwall.
    Corineus brought it thither under one of his arms, they
    say.   230

CHOUGH.

    Oh, Corineus, my predecessor, that I had but liv'd in
    those days to see thee wrestle! On that condition I had
    died seven year ago.

TRIMTRAM.

    Nay, it should have been a dozen at least, i'faith, on that
    condition.   *Exeunt.* 235

[III.i]   *Enter* Captain Ager *with his two* Friends.

CAPTAIN AGER.

    Well, your wills now?

1 AGER'S FRIEND.   Our wills? Our loves, our duties
    To honor'd fortitude; what wills have we
    But our desires to nobleness and merit,
    Valor's advancement, and the sacred rectitude
    Due to a valorous cause?

CAPTAIN AGER.   Oh, that's not mine!   5

2 AGER'S FRIEND.

    War has his court of justice; that's the field
    Where all cases of manhood are determin'd,
    And your case is no mean one.

CAPTAIN AGER [*aside*].   True, then 'twere virtuous;
    But mine is in extremes, foul and unjust.—
    Well, now you've got me hither, you're as far   10
    To seek in your desire as at first minute;
    For by the strength and honor of a vow,
    I will not lift a finger in this quarrel.

1 AGER'S FRIEND.

    How? Not in this? Be not so rash a sinner.

---

10. *hither*] perhaps either Finsbury Fields, a recreation area about
half a mile north of the City walls, or St. George's Fields, southwest
of the City, across the Thames and between Southwark and Lambeth
(Sugden). Both were favored places for duels.

Why, sir, do you ever hope to fight again? 15
Then take heed on't; you must never look for that.
Why, the universal stock of the world's injury
Will be too poor to find a quarrel for you.
Give up your right and title to desert, sir;
If you fail virtue here, she needs you not 20
All your time after; let her take this wrong,
And never presume then to serve her more.
Bid farewell to the integrity of arms,
And let that honorable name of soldier
Fall from you like a shivered wreath of laurel 25
By thunder struck from a desertless forehead,
That wears another's right by usurpation.
Good captain, do not wilfully cast away
At one hour all the fame your life has won;
This is your native seat; here you should seek 30
Most to preserve it. Or if you will dote
So much on life—poor life, which in respect
Of life in honor is but death and darkness—
That you will prove neglectful of yourself,
Which is to me too fearful to imagine, 35
Yet for that virtuous lady's cause, your mother,
Her reputation, dear to nobleness
As grace to penitence, whose fair memory
E'en crowns fame in your issue, for that blessedness,
Give not this ill place; but in spite of hell 40
And all her base fears, be exactly valiant.

CAPTAIN AGER.
Oh, oh, oh!

2 AGER'S FRIEND. Why, well said; there's fair hope in that;
Another such a one.

CAPTAIN AGER. Came they in thousands,
'Tis all against you.

15–16.] *this edn.; in Q1–2 divided* 20. not] *Dyce;* not: *Q1–2.*
then/ that.

---

30. *native seat*] presumably London or an adjoining county; but
possibly all England, contrasted to the Low Countries, where Ager's
exploits were performed.

1 AGER'S FRIEND.   Then, poor friendless merit,
    Heaven be good to thee! Thy professor leaves thee.   45

       Enter the Colonel *and his two* Friends.

    He's come. Do but you draw; we'll fight it for you.
CAPTAIN AGER.
    I know too much to grant that.
1 AGER'S FRIEND.   O dead manhood!
    Had ever such a cause so faint a servant?
    Shame brand me if I do not suffer for him.
COLONEL.
    I've heard, sir, you've been guilty of much boasting   50
    For your brave earliness at such a meeting;
    You've lost the glory of that way this morning;
    I was the first today.
CAPTAIN AGER.   So were you ever
    In my respect, sir.
1 AGER'S FRIEND.   O most base *praeludium*!
CAPTAIN AGER.
    I never thought on victory, our mistress,   55
    With greater reverence than I have your worth,
    Nor ever lov'd her better.
1 AGER'S FRIEND.   'Slight, I could knock
    His brains about his heels, methinks.
2 AGER'S FRIEND.   Peace, prithee, peace.
CAPTAIN AGER.
    Success in you has been my absolute joy;
    And when I have wish'd content, I have wish'd your   60
      friendship.

46. come] *Dyce;* comd *Q1–2.*   57–58. 'Slight . . . methinks] *Dyce;*
                                    printed as prose in Q1–2.

---

46. *we'll fight it*] The code of the duel forbade the seconds to fight,
but they frequently did so, on the pretext of defending their principals' rights (Frederick R. Bryson, *The Sixteenth-Century Italian
Duel* [Chicago, 1938], p. 37).

60. *wish'd your friendship*] The law of the duello forbade any
attempt at reconciliation once the principals had come to the field; see
my Introduction, above, pp. xxiii–xxiv.

1 AGER'S FRIEND.

Stay, let me but run him through the tongue a little;

There's lawyer's blood in't; you shall see foul gear straight.

2 AGER'S FRIEND.

Come, you are as mad now as he's cowardous.

COLONEL.

I came not hither, sir, for an encomium.

1 AGER'S FRIEND.

No, the more coxcomb he, that claws the head   65

Of your vainglory with't!

COLONEL.   I came provided

For storms and tempests and the foulest season

That ever rage let forth, or blew in wildness

From the incensed prison of man's blood.

CAPTAIN AGER.

'Tis otherwise with me; I come with mildness,   70

Peace, constant amity, and calm forgiveness,

The weather of a Christian and a friend.

1 AGER'S FRIEND.

Give me a valiant Turk, though not worth ten pence, rather.

CAPTAIN AGER.

Yet, sir, the world will judge the injury mine,

Insufferable mine, mine beyond injury.   75

Thousands have made a less wrong reach to hell,

Aye, and rejoic'd in his most endless vengeance,

A miserable triumph, though a just one.

But when I call to memory our long friendship,

Methinks it cannot be too great a wrong   80

That then I should not pardon. Why should man,

---

62. *foul gear*] ugly stuff, pus or corruption.

65. *claws the head*] gives comfort by scratching; flatters.

73. *Turk . . . tenpence*] In fields for archery (as at Finsbury) one of the marks set at the shorter distance, 240 paces, was the figure of a Turk. *OED* quotes: "All the rest were but painted posts and Turkes of tenpence to fill and adorne the shooting-field" (1616). Proverbial expression of contempt.

77. *his*] its (i.e., Hell's).

81–87. *Why . . . eternally*] Speaking in general, Ager does not state whether the imagined duellist is defender of the truth; justified or not, the man dies while in the sin of anger and is damned for that.

For a poor hasty syllable or two,
And vented only in forgetful fury,
Chain all the hopes and riches of his soul
To the revenge of that, die lost forever?   85
For he that makes his last peace with his Maker
In anger, anger is his peace eternally;
He must expect the same return again
Whose venture is deceitful. Must he not, sir?

COLONEL.

I see what I must do, fairly put up again;   90
For here'll be nothing done, I perceive that.

CAPTAIN AGER.

What shall be done in such a worthless business
But to be sorry and to be forgiven?
You, sir, to bring repentance, and I pardon.

COLONEL.

I bring repentance, sir?

CAPTAIN AGER.   If it be too much   95
To say repentance, call it what you please, sir;
Choose your own word; I know you're sorry for't,
And that's as good.

COLONEL.   I sorry? By fame's honor, I am wrong'd!
Do you seek for peace, and draw the quarrel larger?

CAPTAIN AGER.

Then 'tis: "I'm sorry that I thought you so."   100

92. business] *Dyce;* businesset *Q1;*   97–98.] *Dyce; in Q1–2 divided:*
businesse *Q2.*   Choose . . . good/ wrong'd.

Ager intends the Colonel to take the moral that both defender and
challenger should put aside anger and seek forgiveness.

88–89. *He . . . deceitful*] an indirect plea for the Colonel to withdraw the insult which Ager now believes to have far more truth than
the Colonel supposes.

94. *pardon*] This word is too injurious to honor to be used in
peace-making even before entry on the field; Ager's use of it shows
his mental agony.

98. *I sorry*] The Colonel's indignation suggests that he regards himself as the "burdened" party, i.e., that Ager has given, or is now
giving him, the lie.

100. *"I'm . . . so"*] the kind of formula recommended by writers
on honor, to be used in making peace; for example, "That which I

1 AGER'S FRIEND.

    A captain? I could gnaw his title off!

CAPTAIN AGER.

    Nor is it any misbecoming virtue, sir,

    In the best manliness to repent a wrong,

    Which made me bold with you.

1 AGER'S FRIEND.

    I could cuff his head off!

2 AGER'S FRIEND.   Nay, pish!

1 AGER'S FRIEND.   Pox on him,   105

    I could eat his buttock bak'd, methinks.

COLONEL [*to his sword*].

    So, once again take thou thy peaceful rest then.

    But as I put thee up, I must proclaim

    This captain here, both to his friends and mine,

    That only came to see fair valor righted,   110

    A base submissive coward; so I leave him.

                                   Offers to go away.

CAPTAIN AGER.

    Oh, heaven has pitied my excessive patience,

    And sent me a cause; now I have a cause!

    A coward I was never. —Come you back, sir!

COLONEL.

    How?

CAPTAIN AGER.   You left a *coward* here?

COLONEL.   Yes, sir, with you.   115

CAPTAIN AGER.

    'Tis such base metal, sir, 'twill not be taken;

    It must home again with you.

2 AGER'S FRIEND.   Should this be true now?

---

said, I thought then to be true [but I was mistaken]" (Sir William Segar, *The Booke of Honor and Armes*, 1590, sig. G3v). (But see the note on l. 60 above.) *So* refers to "son of a whore."

    111. *coward*] Against the rules, but as was often done, the Colonel renews the quarrel on the field after his opponent's refusal to fight; thus he increases his guilt.

    113. *a cause*] a "just cause" or "fair quarrel," in the parlance of honor.

1 AGER'S FRIEND.
>   Impossible! "Coward" do more than "bastard"?
COLONEL.
>   I prithee, mock me not; take heed you do not;
>   For if I draw once more, I shall grow terrible,   120
>   And rage will force me do what will grieve honor.
CAPTAIN AGER.
>   Ha, ha, ha!
COLONEL.
>   He smiles; dare it be he? What think you, gentlemen?
>   Your judgments—shall I not be cozen'd in him?
>   This cannot be the man! Why, he was bookish,   125
>   Made an invective lately against fighting,
>   A thing in troth that mov'd a little with me;
>   Put up a fouler contumely far
>   Than thousand cowards came to, and grew thankful.
CAPTAIN AGER.
>   Blessed remembrance in time of need!   130
>   I'd lost my honor else.
2 AGER'S FRIEND.   Do you note his joy?
CAPTAIN AGER.
>   I never felt a more severe necessity;
>   Then came thy excellent pity. Not yet ready?
>   Have you such confidence in my just manhood
>   That you dare so long trust me, and yet tempt me   135
>   Beyond the toleration of man's virtue?
>   Why, would you be more cruel than your injury?
>   Do you first take pride to wrong me, and then think me
>   Not worth your fury? Do not use me so.
>   I shall deceive you, then. Sir, either draw,   140
>   And that not slightingly, but with the care
>   Of your best preservation; with that watchfulness
>   As you'd defend yourself from circular fire,
>   Your sin's rage, or her lord. This will require it,
>   Or you'll be too soon lost; for I've an anger   145

---

143. *circular fire*] From inside his protective circle of divine symbols the sorcerer raises devils and hell-fire, just outside it.

144. *her lord*] i.e., Satan.

Has gathered mighty strength against you, mighty;
Yet you shall find it honest to the last,
Noble and fair.

COLONEL.   I'll venture't once again;
And if't be but as true as it is wondrous,
I shall have that I come for. Your leave, gentlemen.   150

1 AGER'S FRIEND.

If he should do't indeed, and deceive's all now!
Stay, by this hand, he offers—fights i'faith,
Fights! By this light, he fights, sir!

2 AGER'S FRIEND.   So methinks, sir.

1 AGER'S FRIEND.

An absolute punto, hey?

2 AGER'S FRIEND.   'Twas a passado, sir.

1 AGER'S FRIEND.

Why, let it pass, and 'twas; I'm sure 'twas somewhat.   155
What's that now?

2 AGER'S FRIEND.   That's a punto.

1 AGER'S FRIEND.   Oh, go to, then,
I knew 'twas not far off. What a world's this!
Is "coward" a more stirring meat than "bastard," my masters?
Put in more eggs for shame when you get children,
And make it true court custard. —Ho! I honor thee.   160
                                              Colonel *falls.*

'Tis right and fair; and he that breathes against it,
He breathes against the justice of a man,
And man to cut him off 'tis no injustice.
Thanks, thanks, for this most unexpected nobleness!

CAPTAIN AGER.

Truth never fails her servant, sir, nor leaves him   165
With the day's shame upon him.

150. gentlemen] Gentlemen *Q2;*
Gent. *Q1.*

---

154. *punto*] a stroke or thrust with the point of the sword.
154. *passado*] a step forward with either foot, accompanying a forward thrust of the sword.
160. *court custard*] Quaking custard should be made even more
cowardly (i.e., richer, as at court) so that the eaters' children may more
sharply resent the term "coward."

1 AGER'S FRIEND.   Thou'st redeem'd
　　Thy worth to the same height 'twas first esteem'd.
　　　　　　　　　　　Exeunt Captain Ager *and his* Friends.
1 COLONEL'S FRIEND.
　　Alas, how is it, sir? Give us some hope
　　Of your stay with us. Let your spirit be seen
　　Above your fortune; the best fortitude   170
　　Has been of fate ill-friended. Now force your empire,
　　And reign above your blood, spite of dejection;
　　Reduce the monarchy of your abler mind;
　　Let not flesh straiten it.
COLONEL.   Oh, just heaven has found me,
　　And turn'd the stings of my too hasty injuries   175
　　Into my own blood! I pursu'd my ruin,
　　And urg'd him past the patience of an angel.
　　Could man's revenge extend beyond man's life,
　　This would ha' wak'd it. If this flame will light me
　　But till I see my sister, 'tis a kind one;   180
　　More I expect not from't. Noble deserver!
　　Farewell, most valiant and most wrong'd of men;
　　Do but forgive me, and I am victor then.
　　　　　　　　　　　Exeunt, the Colonel *led by them.*

[III.ii]   *Enter* Physician, Jane, Anne, Dutch Nurse
　　　　　　　　　with the child.

PHYSICIAN.
　　Sweet fro, to your most indulgent care
　　Take this, my heart's joy; I must not tell you
　　The value of this jewel in my bosom.

175. stings] *Dyce;* strings *Q1–2.*

---

　172. *reign . . . blood*] perhaps in two senses, "resist the weakness
caused by loss of blood" and "overcome your passion of despair."
　173. *Reduce*] restore.
　[III.ii]
　0.1 *Dutch*] probably in the sense "German" here, for Rowley follows
closely Giraldi Cinthio's novella, in which, with respect to the
Physician, the nurse is said to be *una sua amante Tedesca* (*De Gli
Hecatommithi* [Venice, 1566], sig. Iilv.) For comic purposes Rowley
endows the Nurse with a dialect (probably conventional) of which
the forms suggest chiefly Dutch or Frisian words.
　1. *fro*] woman, madam (Frisian *frou*).

NURSE.

> Dat you may vell, sir, der can niet forstoore you.

PHYSICIAN.

> Indeed I cannot tell you; you know, nurse,   5
> These are above the quantity of price.
> Where is the glory of the goodliest trees
> But in the fruit and branches? The old stock
> Must decay; and sprigs, scions such as these,
> Must become new stocks from us to glory   10
> In their fruitful issue; so we are made
> Immortal one by other.

NURSE.

> You spreke a most lieben fader, and ick sall do de best of
> tender nurses to dis infant, my pretty frokin.

PHYSICIAN.

> I know you will be loving. Here, sweet friend,   15

Gives money.

> Here's earnest of a large sum of love and coin
> To quit your tender care.

JANE.   I have some reason, too,   *Gives her money.*

> To purchase your dear care unto this infant.

NURSE.

> You be de witness of de baptime, dat is, as you spreken,
> de godimother; ick vell forstoor it so.   20

12. one] *Dyce;* on *Q1–2.*   15.1. *Gives money*] *Dyce;* Giue./
                                money *Q1;* Giue money *Q2.*

---

4. *der . . . you*] probably "who cannot understand you," with
reference to herself (cf. l. 20); less likely (with reference to the baby)
"it cannot grieve you."

4. *der*] who (Dutch).

4. *niet*] not (Dutch).

4. *forstoore*] possibly a corruption of Dutch *verstaan,* "understand,"
or *verstoren,* "disturb, interfere with."

13. *spreke*] speak (Dutch).

13. *lieben*] dear (Frisian *libben?*).

13. *fader*] father (Frisian).

13. *ick*] I (Dutch).

13. *sall*] shall (Frisian *scil?*).

14. *frokin*] girl (Frisian).

15–16. *loving . . . love*] The Physician's effusive tone (cf. l. 1) in
speaking to the Nurse seems to imply a liaison (as in the novella).

JANE.

Yes. —(*Aside*) I am the bad mother, if it be offense.

ANNE.

I must be a little kind, too.   *Gives her money.*

NURSE.

Much tanks to you all; dis child is much beloven, and ick
sall see much care over it.

PHYSICIAN.

Farewell! Good sister, show her the way forth;   25
I shall often visit you, kind nurse.

NURSE.

You sall be velcome.   *Exeunt* Anne *and* Nurse.

JANE.

Oh, sir, what a friend have I found in you!
Where my poor power shall stay in the requital,
Yourself must from your fair condition   30
Make up in mere acceptance of my will.

PHYSICIAN.

Oh, pray you, urge it not! We are not born
For ourselves only; self-love is a sin.
But in our loving donatives to others
Man's virtue best consists; love all begets;   35
Without, all are adulterate and counterfeit.

JANE.

Your boundless love I cannot satisfy
But with a mental memory of your virtues;
Yet let me not engage your cost withal.

21. Yes.—(*Aside*.) I . . . offense.]
Oliphant; Yes, I . . . offence.
Aside. Q1–2, Sampson; Yes, I . . .
mother—if it be offense. (*Aside*.)
Dyce, Bullen.

25. Farewell! Good sister, show
. . . forth;] Farewell.—Good sister,
shew . . . forth.—*Dyce;* Farewell
good sister: Show . . . forth,
Q1–2.

23. *beloven*] beloved (Dutch?).

32–33. *We . . . only*] part of a familiar commonplace occurring
twice in Cicero (*De officiis* 1. 7, and *De finibus* 2. 14), but by Cicero
credited to Plato, *Epistle to Archytas.* Rowley may have read it
recently in Thomas Bretnor's *Almanacke,* 1615, sig. A1v: *Non nobis
solum nati sumus sed partem patria partem parentes &c. vendicant.*
Bretnor is referred to at V.i.129–30.

Beseech you then take restitution   40
Of pains and bounty which you have disburs'd
For your poor debtor.   [*Offers money.*]
PHYSICIAN.   You will not offer it!
Do not esteem my love so mercenary
To be the hire of coin! Sure, I shall think
You do not hold so worthily of me   45
As I wish to deserve.
JANE.   Not recompense!
Then you will beggar me with too much credit.
Is't not sufficient you preserve my name,
Which I had forfeited to shame and scorn,
Cover my vices with a veil of love,   50
Defend and keep me from a father's rage,
Whose love yet infinite (not knowing this)
Might (knowing) turn a hate as infinite?
Sure, he would throw me ever from his blessings,
And cast his curses on me. Yes, further,   55
Your secrecy keeps me in the state of woman;
For else what husband would choose me his wife,
Knowing the honor of a bride were lost?
I cannot number half the good you do me
In the conceal'd retention of my sin;   60
Then make me not worse than I was before,
In my ingratitude, good sir.   [*Offers money.*]
PHYSICIAN.   Again?
I shall repent my love, if you'll so call't,
To be made such a hackney. Give me coin?
I had as lief you gave me poison, lady,   65
For I have art and antidotes 'gainst that;
I might take that, but this I will refuse.
JANE.
Will you then teach me how I may requite you
In some small quantity?

48. Is't] *Dyce;* If *Q1–2.*   68. Will] *Dyce;* Well *Q1–2.*

___

56. *state of woman*] proper state, good reputation (Sampson).
64. *hackney*] drudge.

PHYSICIAN [*aside*].   'Twas that I look'd for.—
   Yes, I will tell you, lady, a full quittance,   70
   And how you may become my creditress.
JANE.
   I beseech you do, sir.
PHYSICIAN.   Indeed I will, lady.
   Not in coin, mistress; for silver, though white,
   Yet it draws black lines. It shall not rule my palm,
   There to mark forth his base corruption.   75
   Pay me again in the same quality
   That I to you tender'd; that's love for love.
   Can you love me, lady? You have confess'd
   My love to you.
JANE.   Most amply.
PHYSICIAN.   Why, faith, then,
   Pay me back that way.
JANE.   How do you mean, sir?   80
PHYSICIAN.
   Tush, our meanings are better understood
   Than shifted to the tongue; it brings along
   A little blabbing blood into our cheeks,
   That shames us when we speak.
JANE.   I understand you not.
PHYSICIAN.
   Fie, you do; make not yourself ignorant   85
   In what you know; you have ta'en forth the lesson
   That I would read to you.
JANE.   Sure, then I need not
   Read it again, sir.
PHYSICIAN.   Yes, it makes perfect.
   You know the way unto Achilles' spear;
   If that hurt you, I have the cure, you see.   90
JANE.
   Come, you're a good man, I do perceive you;

73–74. *silver . . . lines*] proverbial (Tilley, S 459).

86. *ta'en forth*] learned.

89. *Achilles' spear*] the remedy. The wounds made by Achilles'
spear could be healed only by the application of rust taken from it
(H. J. Rose, *A Handbook of Greek Mythology* [New York, 1959], p. 233).

You put a trial to me, I thank you.
You're my just confessor, and, believe me,
I'll have no further penance for this sin.
Convert a year unto a lasting ever,   95
And call't Apollo's smile; 'twas once, then never.

PHYSICIAN.

Pray you, mistake me not; indeed I love you.

JANE.

In deed? What deed?

PHYSICIAN.   The deed that you have done.

JANE.

I cannot believe you.

PHYSICIAN.   Believe the deed, then.

JANE.

Away, you're a blackamoor! You love me?   100
I hate you for your love! Are you the man
That in your painted outside seem'd so white?
Oh, you're a foul, dissembling hypocrite!
You sav'd me from a thief that yourself might rob me,
Skinn'd o'er a green wound to breed an ulcer.   105
Is this the practice of your Physic College?

PHYSICIAN.

Have you yet utter'd all your niceness forth?
If you have more, vent it; certes I think
Your first grant was not yielded with less pain;
If 'twere, you have your price; yield it again.   110

JANE.

Pray you, tell me, sir—I ask'd it before—
Is it a practice 'mongst you physicians?

PHYSICIAN.

Tush, that's a secret; we cast all waters.
Should I reveal, you would mistrust my counsel.

---

100. *blackamoor*] probably "devil" (Sampson), though the earliest citation of this sense in *OED* is of 1663.

106. *practice*] with a pun on the sense "plotting."

107. *niceness*] coyness.

110. *you . . . price*] "say how much you want."

113. *cast all waters*] diagnose all diseases by inspection of urine; here, "know how to deal with all kinds of people."

The lawyer and physician here agrees;   115
To women clients they give back their fees,
And is not that kindness?

JANE.   This for thy love!   *Spits.*
Out, outside of a man! Thou cinnamon tree
That but thy bark hast nothing good about thee!
The unicorn is hunted for his horn,   120
The rest is left for carrion. Thou false man,
Thou'st fish'd with silver hooks and golden baits;
But I'll avoid all thy deceiving sleights.

PHYSICIAN.
Do what you list; I will do something too.
Remember yet what I have done for you;   125
You've a good face now, but 'twill grow rugged
Ere you grow old; old men will despise you.
Think on your grandam Helen, the fairest queen,
When in a new glass she spied her old face;
She, smiling, wept to think upon the change.   130
Take your time; you're craz'd, you're an apple fallen
From the tree; if you be kept long, you'll rot.
Study your answer well; yet I love you.
If you refuse, I have a hand above you.   *Exit* Physician.

126. rugged] *this edn.;* rugged.   134. above you] *Dyce;* aboue. *Q1–*
Q1–2; rugged; *Dyce.*   2.
127. old;] *this edn.;* old: *Q1–2;*
old, *Dyce.*

118–19. *cinnamon tree . . . thee*] A small, shrublike tree, the cinnamon is kept pollarded to force the growth of suckers, which furnish
the aromatic bark, the only useful part of the plant. Jane's metaphor
sounds as if it were proverbial; its truth is vouched for by Thomas
Blundeville in his *Exercises*, 1597, folio 264v. I owe my knowledge of
the passage to Cyrus Hoy.

120–21. *horn . . . carrion*] The unicorn's horn, an antidote for all
poisons and a therapeutic for many other illnesses, was so costly
that few but kings could own it. However, by some accounts the
flesh of the unicorn was too bitter to be eaten (Odell Shepard, *The
Lore of the Unicorn* [New York, 1967], pp. 27, 31, 35).

128–30. *Helen . . . change*] borrowed from Ovid *Metamorphoses* 15.
232; but Rowley (or some other adapter) has modified the image.

131. *Take your time*] "Take advantage of your youth."

131. *craz'd*] impaired.

JANE.

    Poison thyself, thou foul empoisoner;   135
    Of thine own practic drink the theory.
    What a white devil have I met withal!
    What shall I do? What do? Is't a question?
    Nor shame, nor hate, nor fear, nor lust, nor force,
    Now being too bad, shall ever make me worse.   140

Enter Anne.

    What have we here? A second spirit.

ANNE.   Mistress,
    I am sent to you.

JANE.   Is your message good?

ANNE.

    As you receive it; my brother sent me,
    And you know he loves you.

JANE.   I heard say so;
    But 'twas a false report.   145

ANNE.

    Pray, pardon me; I must do my message;
    Who lives commanded must obey his keeper.
    I must persuade you to this act of woman.

JANE.

    Woman! Of strumpet!

ANNE.   Indeed of strumpet;
    He takes you at advantage of your fall,   150
    Seeing you down before.

JANE.   Curse on his feigned smiles!

ANNE.

    He's my brother, mistress, and a curse on you
    If e'er you bless him with that cursed deed!
    Hang him, poison him! He held out a rose

---

136. *practic . . . theory*] possibly means "Use on yourself the malice which actuates your deeds to others."

137. *white devil*] hypocrite.

141. *spirit*] devil.

142. *I am sent*] Sampson plausibly suggests that the Physician is understood to be listening at the back of the stage, and that Anne speaks the lines of her message aloud, but her real opinions *sotto voce*.

To draw the yielding sense, which, come to hand,   155
He shifts, and gives a canker.

JANE.   You speak well yet.

ANNE.

Aye, but, mistress, now I consider it,
Your reputation lies at his mercy;
Your fault dwells in his breast. Say he throw it out,
It will be known. How are you then undone!   160
Think on't, your good name; and they are not to be sold
In every market; a good name's dear,
And indeed more esteemed than our actions,
By which we should deserve it.

JANE.   Ay me, most wretched!

ANNE.

What? Do you shrink at that?   165
Would you not wear one spot upon your face
To keep your whole body from a leprosy,
Though it were undiscover'd ever? Hang him,
Fear him not! Horseleeches suck out his corrupt blood!
Draw you none from him, 'less it be pure and good.   170

JANE.

Do you speak your soul?

ANNE.   By my soul do I.

JANE.

Then yet I have a friend; but thus exhort me,
And I have still a column to support me.

ANNE.

One fault Heaven soon forgives, and 'tis on earth forgot;
The moon herself is not without one spot.   *Exeunt.* 175

[III.iii]   *Enter the* Lady Ager, *meeting her* Servant.

LADY AGER.

Now, sir, where is he? Speak, why comes he not?
I sent you for him! Bless this fellow's senses,
What has he seen? A soul nine hours entranc'd,
Hovering 'twixt hell and heaven, could not wake ghastlier.

---

156. *canker*] wild rose or log-rose.
174. *One fault*] a single sin.

Enter another Servant.

Not yet return an answer? What say you, sir?   5
Where is he?

2 SERVANT.   Gone!

LADY AGER.   What say'st thou?

2 SERVANT.   He is gone, madam.
But as we heard, unwillingly he went
As ever blood enforc'd.

LADY AGER.   Went? Whither went he?

2 SERVANT.
Madam, I fear I ha' said too much already.

LADY AGER.
These men are both agreed. —Speak, whither went he?   10

2 SERVANT.
Why to—I would you'd think the rest yourself, madam.

LADY AGER.
Meek patience bless me!

2 SERVANT.   To the field.

1 SERVANT.   To fight, madam.

LADY AGER.
To fight!

1 SERVANT.   There came two urging gentlemen
That call'd themselves his seconds, both so powerful
As 'tis reported they prevail'd with him   15
With little labor.

LADY AGER.   Oh, he's lost, he's gone!
For all my pains, he's gone; two meeting torrents
Are not so merciless as their two rages.
He never comes again. —[*Aside.*] Wretched affection!
Have I belied my faith, injur'd my goodness,   20
Slander'd my honor for his preservation,

8. he?] *six copies of Q1; five
copies lack the query.*

0.1] This scene offers the only noticeable interruption of the time
sequence of the play; it returns to the hour of the duel, two or three
days before III.ii.

Having but only him, and yet no happier?
'Tis then a judgment plain; truth's angry with me,
In that I would abuse her sacred whiteness
For any worldly temporal respect.   25
Forgive me, then, thou glorious woman's virtue,
Admir'd where'er thy habitation is,
Especially in us weak ones! Oh, forgive me,
For 'tis thy vengeance this. To belie truth,
Which is so hardly ours, with such pain purchas'd,   30
Fastings and prayers, continence and care!
Misery must needs ensue. Let him not die
In that unchaste belief of his false birth
And my disgrace! Whatever angel guides him,
May this request be with my tears obtain'd: 35
Let his soul know my honor is unstain'd.—
Run, seek, away! If there be any hope,   *Exeunt* Servants.
Let me not lose him yet! When I think on him,
His dearness, and his worth, it earns me more;
They that know riches tremble to be poor.   40
My passion is not every woman's sorrow;
She must be truly honest feels my grief,
And only known to one. If such there be,
They know the sorrow that oppresseth me.   *Exit.*

[IV.i]
Enter the Colonel's Second Friend, Usher, Second Roarer, *with*
Chough *and* Trimtram.

25. worldly] *Q2;* wordly *Q1.*	29. this.] *this edn.;* this, *Q1–2;* this! *Dyce.*
[IV.i]	*edn.; Colonels Second Q1–2; Col-*
0.1. Colonel's Second Friend] *this*	*onel's Friend Dyce.*

---

39. *earns*] grieves.
43. *one*] one man (Sampson). The sense of the phrase is "faithful to
one man."

[IV.i]

0.1 *Colonel's Second Friend*] Entitled *Colonels Second* in Q1–2, he
is one of two lieutenants who accompany the Colonel at III.i.46 and
V.i.404.1. In the present scene the Friend appears as an officer out
of employment and funds, living by questionable means.

2 colonel's friend.

> Truth, sir, I must needs blame you for a truant, having
> but one lesson read to you and neglect so soon. Fie! I
> must see you once a day at least.

chough.

> Would I were whipp'd, tutor, if it were not 'long of my
> man Trimtram here.   5

trimtram.

> Who, of me?

chough [*aside to* Trimtram].

> Take't upon thee, Trim. I'll give thee five shillings, as I
> am a gentleman.

trimtram [*to* Chough].

> I'll see you whipp'd first—well, I will too. —Faith, sir, I
> saw he was not perfect, and I was loath he should come   10
> before to shame himself.

2 colonel's friend.

> How? Shame, sir? Is it a shame for scholars to learn? Sir,
> there are great scholars that are but slenderly read in our
> profession. Sir, first it must be economical, then ecu-
> menical. Shame not to practice in the house how to per-   15
> form in the field; the nail that is driven takes a little
> hold at the first stroke, but more at the second, and
> more at the third, but when 'tis home to the head, then
> 'tis firm.

chough.

> Faith, I have been driving it home to the head this two   20
> days.

14. then] *Q1 (corr.);* the *Q1 (un-*
corr.).

0.1 *Usher*] assistant to the head teacher; he may have been an
ensign or corporal.
0.1–2. *Second Roarer*] Q1–2 read *&c.* after *Usher*; but "2 Roarer,"
first speaking at l. 61, suffices to complete the staff of the school
(Colonel's Second Friend is the first roarer). For comment on this
scene see Appendix B.
4. *'long of*] on account of.
14. *economical*] domestic, private.
14–15. *ecumenical*] universal.

TRIMTRAM.

I help'd to hammer it in as well as I could too, sir.

2 COLONEL'S FRIEND.

Well, sir, I will hear you rehearse anon. Meantime peruse
the exemplary of my bills, and tell me in what language
I shall roar a lecture to you; or I'll read to you the mathe- 25
matical science of roaring.

CHOUGH.

Is it mathematical?

2 COLONEL'S FRIEND.

Oh, sir, does not the winds roar? The sea roar? The
welkin roar? Indeed, most things do roar by nature, and
is not the knowledge of these things mathematical?   30

CHOUGH.

Pray proceed, sir.

2 COLONEL'S FRIEND (*reads his bill*).

The names of the languages, the Slavonian, Parthamenian, Barmeothian, Tyburnian, Wappinganian, or the
modern Londonian. Any man or woman that is desirous
to roar in any of these languages, in a week they shall be 35
perfect, if they will take pains; so let 'em repair into
Holborn to the sign of the Cheat Loaf.

CHOUGH.

Now your bill speaks of that. I was wondering a good

25. shall . . . lecture] shal . . .
Lecture *Q1 (corr.);* shall . . . Lec-
tue *Q1 (uncorr.).*

---

24. *exemplary*] copy.

32. *Slavonian*] Slavic or (in common parlance) Russian (Sugden); or
characteristic of abject persons, peasants, rogues (*OED*).

32–33. *Parthamenian*] term of unknown meaning.

33. *Barmeothian*] language of drunken brawls *(barmy oaths,* from
barm, the foam on malt)?

33. *Tyburnian*] from Tyburn, where felons were executed.

33. *Wappinganian*] from Wapping, haunt of sailors, place of execution for pirates.

37. *Cheat Loaf*] Cheat bread, from which the coarsest of the bran
had been removed, was second in quality to manchet; but of the
several grades of cheat, apparently some were fine enough for Court
fare.

while at your sign; the loaf looks very like bread, i'faith,
but why is it called the Cheat Loaf?   40

2 COLONEL'S FRIEND.

This house was sometimes a baker's, sir, that served the
Court, where the bread is called "cheat."

TRIMTRAM.

Aye, aye, 'twas a baker that cheated the Court with bread.

2 COLONEL'S FRIEND.

Well, sir, choose your languages; and your lectures shall
be read between my usher and myself for your better in- 45
struction, provided your conditions be performed in the
premises beforesaid.

CHOUGH.

Look you, sir, there's twenty pound in hand, and twenty
more I am to pay when I am allowed a sufficient roarer.

2 COLONEL'S FRIEND.

You speak in good earnest, sir?   50

CHOUGH.

Yes, faith, do I. Trimtram shall be my witness.

TRIMTRAM.

Yes, indeed, sir, twenty pound is very good earnest.

USHER.

Sir, one thing I must tell you belongs to my place. You
are the youngest scholar, and till another comes under
you, there is a certain garnish belongs to the school. For 55
in our practice we grow to a quarrel; then there must be
wine ready to make all friends, for that's the end of roaring; 'tis valiant but harmless; and this charge is yours.

CHOUGH.

With all my heart, i'faith; and I like it the better because
no blood comes on it. Who shall fetch?   60

2 ROARER.

I'll be your spaniel, sir.

54. comes] *Q1 (corr.); comee Q1
(uncorr.).*

41–43.] The satiric allusion in these lines is obscure.

55. *garnish*] money extorted by the jailer from a new prisoner; as
it were, an entrance fee.

61. S.P. 2 *Roarer*] evidently the lowest in rank of the three ex-
soldiers running the school.

2 COLONEL'S FRIEND.

Bid Vapor bring some tobacco, too.

CHOUGH.

Do, and here's money for't.

USHER [*to* 2 Roarer].

No, you shall not; let me see the money. So, I'll keep it, and discharge him after the combat.   *Exit* 2 Roarer. 65
For your practice' sake you and your man shall roar him out on't, for indeed you must pay your debts so; for that's one of the main ends of roaring; and when you have left him in a chafe, then I'll qualify the rascal.

CHOUGH.

Content, i'faith. Trim, we'll roar the rusty rascal out of 70
his tobacco.

TRIMTRAM.

Aye, and he had the best craccus in London.

2 COLONEL'S FRIEND.

Observe, sir, we could now roar in the Slavonian language; but this practice hath been a little sublime, some hair's-breadth or so above your caput. I take it for your 75
use and understanding both it were fitter for you to taste the modern assault, only the Londonian roar.

CHOUGH.

I'faith, sir, that's for my purpose, for I shall use all my roaring here in London; in Cornwall we are all for wrestling, and I do not mean to travel over sea to roar there. 80

2 COLONEL'S FRIEND.

Observe then, sir; but it were necessary you took forth your tables, to note the most difficult points for the better assistance of your memory.

CHOUGH.

Nay, sir, my man and I keep two tables.

65. S.D.] *Dyce; in Q1–2 S.D. ends*
l. 63.

---

65. *discharge him*] pay the tobacco-seller.
69. *qualify*] mitigate his violence.
72. *craccus*] tobacco from Caracas, Venezuela (Brooks, 2:43).
82. *tables*] memorandum book, tablet.

TRIMTRAM.

Aye, sir, and as many trenchers; cat's meat and dog's meat   85
enough.

2 COLONEL'S FRIEND.

Note, sir —Dost thou confront my cyclops?

USHER.

With a Briarean brousted.

CHOUGH [*writing*].

Cyclops.

TRIMTRAM [*writing*].

Briarean.   90

2 COLONEL'S FRIEND.

I know thee and thy lineal pedigree.

USHER.

It is collateral, as Brutus and Posthumus.

TRIMTRAM.

Brutus.

CHOUGH.

Posthumus.

2 COLONEL'S FRIEND.

False as the face of Hecate; thy sister is a—   95

USHER.

What is my sister, centaur?

2 COLONEL'S FRIEND.

I say thy sister is a bronstrops.

---

87. *cyclops*] sword? But in the Additions (Appendix A below), ll.
61, 100, the meaning seems to be "man" or "swordsman."

88. *Briarean*] like the hundred-handed Titan.

88. *brousted*] possibly *brust-head*, "bristly head."

92. *collateral . . . Posthumus*] Some writers held that Brut's father,
Silvius Posthumus, was the son of Ascanius (whose father was Aeneas);
others held that he was the half-brother of Ascanius (as in the
Aeneid 6. 763–65).

95. *False . . . Hecate*] Statues of Hecate had three faces (or heads):
one her own, another Selene's, another Artemis's *(Aeneid* 4. 511); but
the identity of any one might be doubtful.

96. *centaur*] pimp (as in the Additions, ll. 57–58)? or roarer?

97. *bronstrops*] bawd or harlot; see the Additions, l. 183. Rather than
being a corruption of "bawdstrott," as has been suggested, this word
was coined by Rowley from the names of two Cyclops in the *Aeneid*
8, 424–25. *Ferrum exercebant vasto Cyclopes in antro,/ Brontesque
Steropesque et nudus membra Pyracmon.*

USHER.

A bronstrops!

CHOUGH.

Tutor, tutor, ere you go any further, tell me the English
of that. What is a bronstrops, pray?   100

2 COLONEL'S FRIEND.

A bronstrops is in English a hippocrene.

CHOUGH.

A hippocrene; note it, Trim. I love to understand the
English as I go.

TRIMTRAM.

What's the English of hippocrene?

CHOUGH.

Why, bronstrops!   105

USHER.

Thou dost obtrect my flesh and blood.

2 COLONEL'S FRIEND.

Again I denounce, thy sister is a fructifer.

CHOUGH.

What's that, tutor?

2 COLONEL'S FRIEND.

That is in English a fucus or a minotaur.

CHOUGH.

A minotaur.   110

TRIMTRAM.

A fucus.

USHER.

I say thy mother is a callicut, a panagron, a duplar, and
a sindicus.

111. S.P. TRIMTRAM] *Dyce*; *Chau.*
Q1; *Sec. Q2.*

---

101. *hippocrene*] harlot.
106. *obtrect*] disparage.
107. *fructifer*] harlot, "pleasure-bringer"; apparently Rowley's coin-
age.
109. *fucus*] rouge (but here "harlot").
109. *minotaur*] probably used here, like *centaur*, l. 96, to suggest a
rhyme with "whore."
112. *callicut*] used for the bawdy allusion, without reference to
the city.

2 COLONEL'S FRIEND.

Dislocate thy bladud!

USHER.

Bladud shall conjure if his demons once appear.   115

Enter 2 Roarer *with wine, and* Vapor *with tobacco.*

2 COLONEL'S FRIEND.

Advance thy respondency!

CHOUGH.

Nay, good gentleman, do not fall out. A cup of wine
quickly, Trimtram!

USHER.

See, my steel hath a glister!

CHOUGH.

Pray wipe him, and put him up again, good usher.   120

USHER.

Sir, at your request I pull down the flag of defiance.

2 COLONEL'S FRIEND.

Give me a bowl of wine; my fury shall be quench'd. Here,
usher.

USHER.

I pledge thee in good friendship.

CHOUGH.

I like the conclusion of roaring very well, i'faith.   125

TRIMTRAM.

It has an excellent conclusion indeed if the wine be good,
always provided.

2 COLONEL'S FRIEND.

Oh, the wine must be always provided, be sure of that.

---

112. *panagron*] Sampson suggests the meaning "catch-all."

112. *duplar*] one who gets a double allowance (rare legal term).

113. *sindicus*] A *syndicus* is one who is deputed to transact legal
affairs; but here the word may be used for its first syllable.

114. *Dislocate thy bladud*] "Draw thy sword" (Dyce). The legend
of King Bladud's broken neck seems irrelevant here. Bladud, son of
Lud, was a pre-Roman king of Britain who became a sorcerer and
attempted to fly, but fell to his death (Thomas Beard, *The Theatre
of Gods Iudgements*, 1597, sig. Iiv).

116. *Advance thy respondency*] "Raise your weapon."

USHER.

　　Else you spoil the conclusion, and that, you know, crowns
　　all.　　　　　　　　　　　　　　　　　　　　　　　　　130

CHOUGH.

　　'Tis much like wrestling, i'faith, for we shake hands ere
　　we begin; now that's to avoid the law, for then if he
　　throw him a furlong into the ground, he cannot recover
　　himself upon him, because 'twas done in cold friendship.

2 COLONEL'S FRIEND.

　　I believe you, sir.　　　　　　　　　　　　　　　　135

CHOUGH.

　　And then we drink afterwards, just in this fashion;
　　wrestling and roaring are as like as can be, i'faith, even
　　like long sword and half pike.

2 COLONEL'S FRIEND.

　　Nay, they are reciprocal, if you mark it; for as there is a
　　great roaring at wrestling, so there is a kind of wrestling 140
　　and contention at roaring.

CHOUGH.

　　True, i'faith, for I have heard 'em roar from the six wind-
　　mills to Islington. Those have been great falls then.

2 COLONEL'S FRIEND.

　　Come, now a brief rehearsal of your other day's lesson,
　　betwixt your man and you, and then for today we break 145
　　up school.

CHOUGH.

　　Come, Trimtram. —If I be out, tutor, I'll be bold to look
　　in my tables, because I doubt I am scarce perfect.

2 COLONEL'S FRIEND.

　　Well, well, I will not see small faults.

144. S.P. 2 COLONEL'S FRIEND]
COL.'S FR. *Dyce; Ser. Q1–2. So also*
at l. 149 S.P. and l. 158 S.P.

142–43. *six windmills*] in Finsbury Fields. To the north lay the rural
area of Islington, used by Londoners for recreation (the distance
meant may be about a mile).
　　149. *will . . . faults*] The proverb "Wink at small faults" is the
motto for 19 August in Bretnor's *Almanacke* of 1617.

CHOUGH [*jostling* Trimtram].

    The wall!　　　　　　　　　　　　　　　　　150

TRIMTRAM.

    The wall of me? To thy kennel, spaniel!

CHOUGH.

    Wilt thou not yield precedency?

TRIMTRAM.

    To thee? I know thee and thy brood.

CHOUGH.

    Know'st thou my brood? I know thy brood, too; thou art
    a rook.　　　　　　　　　　　　　　　　　155

TRIMTRAM.

    The nearer akin to the choughs!

CHOUGH.

    The rooks akin to the choughs!

2 COLONEL'S FRIEND.

    Very well maintain'd.

CHOUGH.

    Dungcoer, thou liest!

TRIMTRAM.

    Lie! Enucleate the kernel of thy scabbard!　　　160

CHOUGH.

    Now if I durst draw my sword, 'twere valiant, i'faith.

2 COLONEL'S FRIEND.

    Draw, draw, howsoever.

CHOUGH.

    Have some wine ready to make us friends, I pray you.

TRIMTRAM.

    Chough, I will make thee fly and roar!

CHOUGH.

    I will roar if thou strik'st me!　　　　　　　165

157. choughs] Chaughs *Q1 (corr.);*
Chaughis *Q1 (uncorr.).*

---

  150. *The wall*] i.e., "Give me the wall."
  151. *kennel*] channel, gutter in the middle of the street.
  159. *Dungcoer*] possibly a compositor's error, meant for "Dungcock"
(i.e., dunghill cock), though a double mistake of *er* for *ck* is unlikely.
  160. *Enucleate*] extract the kernel from. See the Additions, l. 82.

2 COLONEL'S FRIEND.

So, 'tis enough; now conclude in wine. I see you will
prove an excellent practitioner. Wondrous well perform'd on both sides.

CHOUGH.

Here, Trimtram, I drink to thee.

TRIMTRAM.

I'll pledge you in good friendship.   170

Enter a Servant.

SERVANT.

Is there not one master Chough here?

USHER.

This is the gentleman, sir.

SERVANT.

My master, sir, your elected father-in-law, desires speedily
to speak with you.

CHOUGH.

Friend, I will follow thee; I would thou hadst come a 175
little sooner, thou shouldst have seen roaring sport,
i'faith.

SERVANT.

Sir, I'll return that you are following.   *Exit* Servant.

CHOUGH.

Do so. I'll tell thee, tutor, I am to marry shortly; but I
will defer it a while till I can roar perfectly, that I may 180
get the upper hand of my wife on the wedding day; 't
must be done at first or never.

2 COLONEL'S FRIEND.

'Twill serve you to good use in that, sir.

CHOUGH [*to* Vapor].

How lik'st thou this, whiffler?

167. excellent] *Q1 (corr.)*; exce-   in *Q1 (corr.)*; pldge in *Q1 (un-*
lent *Q1 (uncorr.)*.   *corr.)*.
170. pledge you in] *Q2;* pldge you   171. Chough] *Chaugh Q1 (corr.)*;
                                           Chauogh Q1 (uncorr.).

---

184. *whiffler*] piper of music in a procession; hence, smoker of a
tobacco pipe.

VAPOR.

Very valiantly, i'faith, sir.   185

CHOUGH.

Tush, thou shalt see more by and by.

VAPOR.

I can stay no longer indeed, sir. Who pays me for my
tobacco?

CHOUGH.

How, pay for tobacco? Away, ye sooty-mouth'd piper!
You rusty piece of Martlemas bacon, away!   190

TRIMTRAM.

Let me give him a mark for't.

CHOUGH.

No, Trimtram, do not strike him; we'll only roar out a
curse upon him.

TRIMTRAM.

Well, do you begin then.

CHOUGH.

May thy roll rot, and thy pudding drop in pieces, being 195
sophisticated with filthy urine!

TRIMTRAM.

May sergeants dwell on either side of thee, to fright away
thy two-penny customers!

CHOUGH.

And for thy penny ones, let them suck thee dry!

TRIMTRAM.

When thou art dead, mayst thou have no other sheets to 200
be buried in but moldy tobacco leaves!

CHOUGH.

And no strewings to stick thy carcass but the bitter stalks!

TRIMTRAM.

Thy mourners all greasy tapsters!

---

190. *Martlemas bacon*] St. Martin's day, 11 November, was the
traditional date for salting the winter's meat.

191. *mark*] (1) a cut or bruise with the sword and (2) a "money of
account" (not an actual coin) of 13*s*. 4*d*.

195. *roll*] tobacco leaves twisted into a thin rope.

195. *pudding*] "small rolls of compressed tobacco treated with mo-
lasses or wine, etc." (Brooks, 2: 43; 4: 401).

202. *strewings*] commonly of rosemary.

CHOUGH.

With foul tobacco pipes in their hats instead of rotten
rosemary; and, last of all, may my man and I live to see 205
all this perform'd, and to piss reeking even upon thy
grave.

TRIMTRAM.

And last of all for me, let this epitaph be remembered
over thee:

> Here coldly now within is laid to rot   210
> A man that yesterday was piping hot.
> Some say he died by pudding, some by prick,
> Others by roll and ball, some leaf; all stick
> Fast in censure, yet think it strange and rare,
> He liv'd by smoke, yet died for want of air!   215
> But then the surgeon said when he beheld him,
> "It was the burning of his pipe that kill'd him."

CHOUGH.

So, are you paid now, whiffler?

VAPOR.

All this is but smoke out of a stinking pipe.

CHOUGH.

So, so, pay him now, usher.   220

2 COLONEL'S FRIEND.

Do not henceforth neglect your schooling, master Chough.

CHOUGH.

Call me rook if I do, tutor.

TRIMTRAM.

And me raven, though my name be Trimtram.

211. *yesterday*] *Q1 (corr.); yester-*   226. trumpets] *Dyce;* trumpet *Q1–*
bay Q1 (uncorr.).   *2.*
212. *say*] *Q1 (corr.); sap Q1 (un-*
corr.).

---

212. *prick*] an established quantity of tobacco.
213. *ball*] tobacco coarsely spun into a thick twist, which was then
rolled into balls (Brooks, 4: 395).
214. *censure*] judgment.
217. *burning*] infection by venereal disease.
217. *pipe*] *OED* does not give the sense "penis," evidently intended
here.

CHOUGH.

Farewell, tutor.

TRIMTRAM.

Farewell, usher.   225

[*Exeunt* Chough *and* Trimtram.]

2 COLONEL'S FRIEND.

Thus when the drum's unbrac'd, and trumpets cease,
Soldiers must get pay for to live in peace.   *Exeunt* Roarers.

[IV.ii]

Enter the Colonel's Sister, *meeting the* Surgeon; [*the* Colonel *discovered in bed, his* 1 Friend *seated nearby*].

COLONEL'S SISTER.

Oh, my most worthy brother, thy hard fate 'twas!
Come hither, honest surgeon, and deal faithfully
With a distressed virgin. What hope is there?

SURGEON.

Hope? *Chillis* was 'scap'd miraculously, lady.

COLONEL'S SISTER.

What's that, sir?   5

SURGEON.

Cava vena. I care but little for his wound i'th' orsophag,
not thus much, trust me; but when they come to *dia-phragma* once, the small intestines, or the spinal medul,

0.1–2. *the* Colonel . . . *nearby*]
*this edn.; Dyce includes "several
friends" watching the Colonel.*

0.1–2. *Colonel discovered*] Probably curtains on the rear stage wall
are opened, and the Colonel's bed is revealed or thrust forward; the
Sister draws the Surgeon aside for questioning.

4. *Chillis*] *cava vena*, the vein which runs from the lower abdomen
to the liver (Helkiah Crooke, *Microcosmographia*, 1618, sigs. L3v–L4r).
On the satiric portrayal of the Surgeon, see George R. Price, "Medical
Men in *A Fair Quarrel*," *Bulletin of the History of Medicine* 24 (1950):
38–42.

6. *orsophag*] the oesophagus?

8. *spinal medul*] "The inner substance of a nerve is medullous, the
outward membranous" (Crooke, *Microcosmographia*, sig. D4v).

or i'th' roots of the emunctories of the noble parts, then
straight I fear a syncops; the flanks retiring towards the   10
back, the urine bloody, the excrements purulent, and the
dolor pricking or pungent.

COLONEL'S SISTER.

Alas, I'm ne'er the better for this answer.

SURGEON.

Now, I must tell you his principal dolor lies i'th' region
of the liver, and there's both inflammation and turma-   15
faction fear'd. Marry, I made him a quadragular plumation, where I used *sanguis draconis*, by my faith, with
powders incarnative, which I temper'd with oil of hypericon and other liquors mundificative.

COLONEL'S SISTER

Pox o' your mundies figatives, I would they were all   20
fired!

SURGEON.

But I purpose, lady, to make another experiment at next

---

9. *emunctories*] any part of the body whose function is to purge
or cleanse a major organ.

9. *noble parts*] the brain, the heart, and the liver (some writers add
the testicles); the ignoble parts minister to them; most ignobly, the
emunctories (Crooke, *Microcosmographia*, sigs. D4r–D4v).

10. *syncops*] syncope, "a sodaine decaye of strength" (Gale, sig. G6r).

11. *excrements*] discharges from the wound.

12. *dolor*] pain.

15–16. *turmafaction*] blunder for "tumefaction," morbid swelling.
John Woodall mentions tumor as a complication to be feared after
wounds in the liver (along with bloody discharges, inflammation, and
fever) (*The Surgions Mate*, 1617, sig. S1r).

16. *quadragular*] blunder for "quadrangular."

16–17. *plumation*] plumaciol, pledget.

17. *sanguis draconis*] dragon's blood; a red resin of *Calamus draco*,
a climbing palm. Used very commonly in medicine, as for cicatrizing
(Arturo Castiglioni, *A History of Medicine* [New York, 1947], p. 384).

18. *powders incarnative*] used to foster the growth of flesh; but if
the wound is inflamed (l. 15), a wiser doctor would consider this treat-
ment premature. Among such incarnatives are colophonia and un-
guentum aureum (Gale, *Certaine Workes*, sigs. A7v, C6v, L1r).

18–19. *hypericon*] hypericum (Saint-John's-wort), i.e., the extract,
oil of hypericon, regarded as a panacea.

19. *liquors mundificative*] cleansing liniments.

22. *experiment*] trial.

dressing with a sarcotric medicament made of iris of
Florence, thus: mastic, calaphena, apopanax, sacrocolla.

COLONEL'S SISTER.

Sacro-halter! What comfort is i'this to a poor gentle-   25
woman? Pray tell me in plain terms what you think of
him.

SURGEON.

Marry, in plain terms I know not what to say to him.
The wound, I can assure you, inclines to paralism, and
I find his body cacochemic; being then in fear of fever   30
and inflammation, I nourish him altogether with viands
refrigerative and give for potion the juice of savicola
dissolv'd with water cerefolium. I could do no more,
lady, if his best guiguimos were dissevered.   *Exit.*

COLONEL'S SISTER.

What thankless pains does the tongue often take   35
To make the whole man most ridiculous!
I come to him for comfort, and he tires me
Worse than my sorrow. What a precious good
May be delivered sweetly in few words!
And what a mount of nothing has he cast forth!   40
Alas, his strength decays! —How cheer you, sir,
My honor'd brother?

---

23. *sarcotric*] blunder for "sarcotic," i.e., incarnative.

24. *mastic*] resin from a Mediterranean tree of the sumac family;
widely used in liniments and unguents.

24. *calaphena*] probably colophonia, resin distilled from turpentine.

24. *apopanax*] i.e., opopanax, a gum-resin made from the juice of
the roots of a southern European herb; used as an anti-spasmodic.

24. *sacrocolla*] blunder for "sarcocolla," a gum-resin from Persia;
used to agglutinate wounds.

29. *paralism*] The Surgeon's meaning is obscure; this word does
not seem to occur elsewhere, and if it is a blunder for "paralysis,"
that term is inapplicable to wounds.

30. *cacochemic*] having unhealthy or depraved humors.

32. *savicola*] not recorded in *OED* or Gale's antidotary in *Certaine
Workes*. Possibly intended for "salvia," or sage; the Surgeon uses it
in a broth.

33. *cerefolium*] chervil, a pot herb.

34. *guiguimos*] blunder for "ginglymus," a "diarthrodial joint."

COLONEL.   In soul never better.
    I feel an excellent health there, such a stoutness;
    My invisible enemy flies me, seeing me arm'd
    With penitence and forgiveness. They fall backward,   45
    Whether through admiration, not imagining
    There were such armory in a soldier's soul
    As pardon and repentance, or through power
    Of ghostly valor—but I have been lord
    Of a more happy conquest in nine hours now   50
    Than in nine years before. Oh, kind lieutenant,
    This is the only war we should provide for,
    Where he that forgives largest and sighs strongest
    Is a tried soldier, a true man in deed,
    And wins the best field, makes his own heart bleed.   55
    Read the last part of that will, sir.

1 COLONEL'S FRIEND (*reads*).

    I also require at the hands of my most beloved sister,
    whom I make full executrix, the disposure of my body in
    burial at St. Martin's i'th' Field; and to cause to be dis-
    tributed to the poor of the same parish forty mark, and   60
    to the hospital of maimed soldiers a hundred. Lastly I
    give and bequeath to my kind, dear, and virtuous sister
    the full possession of my present estate in riches, whether
    it be in lands, leases, money, goods, plate, jewels, or what
    kind soever, upon this condition following, that she   65
    forthwith tender both herself and all these infeoffments
    to that noble captain, my late enemy, Captain Ager.

COLONEL'S SISTER.

    How, sir?

COLONEL.

    Read it again, sir; let her hear it plain.

COLONEL'S SISTER.

    Pray, spare your pains, sir; 'tis too plain already.   70
    Good sir, how do you? Is your memory perfect?

51. lieutenant] *this edn.;* lieuten-   57. S.P. 1 COLONEL'S FRIEND] *Dyce;*
ants *Q1–2.*   1 *Liefetenant Q1–2.*

53. *he . . . strongest*] Apparently the Colonel speaks impersonally
of two qualities of any genuine Christian, to forgive injuries received
and to grieve for wrongs committed.

This will makes question of you; I bestow'd
So much grief and compassion o' your wound,
I never look'd into your senses' epilepsy.
The sickness and infirmity of your judgment   75
Is to be doubted now, more than your body's.
Why, is your love no dearer to me, sir,
Than to dispose me so upon the man
Whose fury is your body's present torment?
The author of your danger? One I hate   80
Beyond the bounds of malice! Do you not feel
His wrath upon you? I beseech you, sir,
Alter that cruel article.
COLONEL.   Cruel sister!—
Forgive me, natural love; I must offend thee,
Speaking to this woman. —Am I content,   85
Having much kindred, yet to give thee all,
Because in thee I'd raise my means to goodness;
And canst thou prove so thankless to my bounty,
To grudge my soul her peace? Is my intent
To leave her rich, whose only desire is   90
To send me poorer into the next world
Than ever usurer went or politic statist?
Is it so burdensome for thee to love
Where I forgive? Oh, wretched is the man
That builds the last hopes of his saving comforts   95
Upon a woman's charity! He's most miserable;
If it were possible, her obstinate will
Will pull him down in his midway to heaven.
I've wrong'd that worthy man past recompense
And in my anger robb'd him of fair fame;   100
And thou the fairest restitution art
My life could yield him; if I knew a fairer,

---

74. *senses' epilepsy*] The Sister speaks inexactly; for any absurdity
in the Colonel's will must be due to coma or lethargy of the rational
soul, not of the internal senses (common sense, imagination, memory).
101. *fairest restitution*] The Colonel wishes to redress the wrong
done to Ager's reputation by uniting his own blood to Ager's. Parallels
for this offering of the Sister occur in Spanish drama and story; see
Eleanor F. Jourdain, *An Introduction to French Classical Drama* (Oxford, 1912), p. 73.

I'd set thee by and thy unwilling goodness,
And never make my sacred peace of thee.
But there's the cruelty of a fate debarr'd;   105
Thou art the last, and all, and thou art hard.

COLONEL'S SISTER.

Let your griev'd heart hold better thoughts of me.
I will not prove so, sir, but since you enforce it
With such a strength of passion, I'll perform
What by your will you have enjoin'd me to,   110
Though the world never show me joy again.

COLONEL.

Oh, this may be fair cunning for the time,
To put me off, knowing I hold not long;
And when I look to have my joys accomplish'd,
I shall find no such things. That were vild cozenage,   115
And not to be repented.

COLONEL'S SISTER.   By all the blessedness
Truth and a good life looks for, I will do't, sir.

COLONEL.

Comforts reward you for't whene'er you grieve;
I know if you dare swear, I may believe.
            [*Exit* Colonel's Sister. *A curtain conceals Colonel's bed.*]

[IV.iii]   *Enter* Captain Ager.

CAPTAIN AGER.

No sooner have I entrance i'this house now
But all my joy falls from me, which was wont
To be the sanctuary of my comforts.
Methought I lov'd it with a reverent gladness,
As holy men do consecrated temples,   5
For the saint's sake which I believ'd my mother;
But prov'd a false faith since, a fearful heresy.
Oh, who'd erect th'assurance of his joys
Upon a woman's goodness? Whose best virtue
Is to commit unseen, and highest secrecy   10
To hide but her own sin; there's their perfection.
And if she be so good, which many fail of, too,

---

12. *if . . . good*] "if my mother has achieved the perfection of hiding her sin."

When these are bad, how wondrous ill are they!
What comfort is't to fight, win this day's fame,
When all my after days are lamps of shame?   15

Enter the Lady Ager.

LADY AGER.
Blessings be firm to me, he's come! 'Tis he!
A surgeon speedily!
CAPTAIN AGER.   A surgeon? Why, madam?
LADY AGER.
Perhaps you'll say 'tis but a little wound!
Good to prevent a danger. —Quick, a surgeon!
CAPTAIN AGER.
Why, madam?   20
LADY AGER.
Aye, aye, that's all the fault of valiant men;
They'll not be known o' their hurts till they're past help,
And then too late they wish for't.
CAPTAIN AGER.   Will you hear me?
LADY AGER.
'Tis no disparagement to confess a wound;
I'm glad, sir, 'tis no worse—a surgeon quickly!   25
CAPTAIN AGER.
Madam—
LADY AGER.   Come, come, sir, a wound's honorable,
And never shames the wearer.
CAPTAIN AGER.   By the justice
I owe to honor, I came off untouch'd.
LADY AGER.
I'd rather believe that!
CAPTAIN AGER.   You believe truth so.
LADY AGER.
My tears prevail, then. Welcome, welcome, sir,   30
As peace and mercy to one new departed!
Why would you go, though, and deceive me so,
When my abundant love took all the course

16. S.P. LADY AGER] *La. Q2; not
in Q1.*

That might be to prevent it? I did that
For my affection's sake (goodness forgive me for't!)   35
That were my own life's safety put upon't,
I'd rather die than do't. Think how you us'd me, then,
And yet would you go, and hazard yourself too!
'Twas but unkindly done.

CAPTAIN AGER.   What's all this, madam?

LADY AGER.

    See, then, how rash you were and short in wisdom!   40
Why, wrong my faith I did, slander'd my constancy,
Belied my truth; that which few mothers will,
Or fewer can, I did, out of true fear
And loving care, only to keep thee here.

CAPTAIN AGER.

    I doubt I am too quick of apprehension now,   45
And that's a general fault, when we hear joyfully.
With the desire of longing for't, I ask it:
Why, were you never false?

LADY AGER.   May death come to me
    Before repentance then!

CAPTAIN AGER.   I heard it plain, sure.
    Not false at all?

LADY AGER.   By the reward of truth,   50
    I never knew that deed that claims the name on't.

CAPTAIN AGER.

    May, then, that glorious reward you swore by
Be never failing to you! All the blessings
That you have given me since obedient custom
Taught me to kneel and ask 'em, are not valuable   55
With this immaculate blessing of your truth.
This is the palm to victory,   [Kneels.]
The crown for all deserts past and to come.
Let 'em be numberless; they are rewarded,
Already they're rewarded! Bless this frame;   60
I feel it much too weak to bear the joy on't.

LADY AGER.

    Rise, sir!

51.] *Dyce; in Q1–2 divided* deed/
on't.

CAPTAIN AGER.   Oh, pardon me—
    I cannot honor you too much, too long;
    I kneel not only to a mother now,
    But to a woman that was never false.   65
    You're dear, and you're good, too; I think o' that.
    What reverence does she merit! 'Tis fit such
    Should be distinguish'd from the prostrate sex,
    And what distinction properer can be shown
    Than honor done to her that keeps her own?   70
LADY AGER.
    Come, sir, I'll have you rise.
CAPTAIN AGER.   To do a deed, then,   *Rises.*
    That shall for ever raise me. O my glory,
    Why, this, this is the quarrel that I look'd for;
    The tother but a shift to hold time play.
    You sacred ministers of preservation,   75
    For heaven's sake send him life,
    And with it mighty health, and such a strength
    May equal but the cause! I wish no foul things.
    If life but glow in him, he shall know instantly
    That I'm resolv'd to call him to account for't.   80
LADY AGER.
    Why, hark you, sir!
CAPTAIN AGER.   I bind you by your honor,
    Madam, you speak no hindrance to't; take heed,
    You ought not.
LADY AGER.
    What an unhappiness have I in goodness!
    'Tis ever my desire to intend well,   85
    But have no fortunate way in't. For all this

81–83. I . . . not] *this edn.; Dyce*   not. *The final* t *of* too't *is blurred*
divides at honour, madam,/ not.;   *in Q1; hence Dyce's reading* to's.
Q1–2 at honor, Madame,/ too't,/

---

74. *shift . . . play*] "a contrivance to keep time occupied" i.e., to
gain time. (The idiom was "to hold someone in play.") But Ager's
figurative language does not mean that his attempt at reconciliation
(III.i.53–104) was in fact a provocation; see Introduction, above, pp.
xxiii-xxiv. One cannot conceive for what purpose he would be trying
to "gain time" when he fought the duel.

Deserve I yet no better of you, but to be griev'd again?
Are you not well with honest gain of fame,
With safety purchas'd? Will you needs tempt a ruin
That avoids you?   *Exit* Lady Ager.   90
CAPTAIN AGER.
No, you've prevail'd; things of this nature sprung,
When they use action must use little tongue.

                    Enter a Servant.

Now, sir, the news?
SERVANT.   Sir, there's a gentlewoman
Desires some conference with you.
CAPTAIN AGER.   How, with me?
A gentlewoman? What is she?
SERVANT.   Her attendant   95
Delivered her to be the Colonel's sister.   [*Exit* Servant.]
CAPTAIN AGER.
Oh, for a storm, then! 'Las, poor virtuous gentlewoman,
I will endure her violence with much pity.
She comes to ease her heart, good noble soul;
'Tis e'en a charity to release the burden.   100
Were not that remedy ordain'd for women,
Their hearts would never hold three years together.
And here she comes. I never mark'd so much of her;
                    Enter the Colonel's Sister.
That face can be the mistress of no anger
But I might very well endure a month, methinks.—   105
I am the man; speak, lady; I'll stand fair.

92.1.] *Dyce; in Q1–2 centered be-*
low news, *l. 93.*

97.] *Dyce; in Q1–2 divided* then/
gentlewoman.

---

88. *honest . . . fame*] Ager's victory has confirmed his own and
Lady Ager's honor, if Ager is regarded as challenger; but whether
challenger or defender, he has increased his acquired honor.
91. *things . . . sprung*] probably quarrels in general; otherwise,
quarrels involving a woman's reputation.
92. *When . . . tongue*] "Should be settled by quick action, with few
words." To renew the quarrel about the slander would be to raise
public doubt about her virtue. And to take the field against a man
already dishonored by defeat was against the code (*Vincentio Saviolo
His Practise*, 1595, sig. Ee4r).

COLONEL'S SISTER.

And I'm enjoin'd by vow to fall thus low   *She kneels.*
And from the dying hand of a repentant
Offer for expiation of wrongs done you,
Myself, and with myself all that was his,   110
Which upon that condition was made mine,
Being his soul's wish to depart absolute man,
In life a soldier, death a Christian.

CAPTAIN AGER.

Oh, heaven has touch'd him nobly! How it shames
My virtue's slow perfection! Rise, dear brightness,   115
I forget manners, too; up, matchless sweetness.

COLONEL'S SISTER.

I must not, sir; there is not in my vow
That liberty; I must be receiv'd first,
Or all denied. If either, I am free.

CAPTAIN AGER.

He must be without soul should deny thee;   120
And with that reverence I receive the gift
As it was sent me. Worthy Colonel
Has such a conquering way i'th' blest things!
Whoever overcomes, he only wins.   *Exeunt.*

[V.i]   *Enter* Physician *and* Jane *as a bride.*

PHYSICIAN.

Will you be obstinate?

JANE.   Torment me not,
Thou ling'ring executioner to death,

124. *Exeunt*] Dyce; *Exit Q1–2. At*   *remaining copies after most of the*
this point in Q1 (between leaves   *edition had been sold. In the*
H3 and H4) three leaves bearing   *present edition the Additions are*
the Additions were inserted in   *placed in Appendix A.*

---

112. *absolute man*] in two senses, "complete" and "absolved."
115. *perfection*] perfecting, growth toward perfection.

[V.i]
2. *ling'ring executioner*] The Physician is compared to a hangman
who moves too slowly in his task of cutting down the felon (half-
strangled in the noose) and disemboweling him.

Greatest disease to nature, that striv'st by art
To make men long a-dying! Your practice is
Upon men's bodies. As men pull roses   5
For their own relish, but to kill the flower,
So you maintain your lives by others' deaths.
What eat you then but carrion?
PHYSICIAN.   Fie, bitterness,
You'd need to candy o'er your tongue a little;
Your words will hardly be digested else.   10
JANE.
You can give yourself a vomit to return 'em
If they offend your stomach.
PHYSICIAN.   Hear my vow.
You are to be married today.
JANE.   A second torment,
Worse than the first, 'cause unavoidable!
I would I could as soon annihilate   15
My father's will in that as forbid thy lust.
PHYSICIAN.
If you then tender an unwilling hand,
Meet it with revenge; marry a cuckold.
JANE.
If thou wilt marry me, I'll make that vow
And give my body for satisfaction   20
To him that should enjoy me for his wife.
PHYSICIAN.
Go to, I'll mar your marriage!
JANE.   Do, plague me so.
I'll rather bear the brand of all that's past
In capital characters upon my brow
Than think to be thy whore or marry him.   25

8. but] *Dyce;* by *Q1–2.*

---

14. *the first*] the Physician's pursuit of her.
18. *it*] Russell's enforcement of the marriage.
21. *him*] Fitzallen; but the Physician probably thinks she means Chough.
24. *capital characters*] A sinner condemned to public penance often wore a paper band or cap with a label in capital letters; in this case "Fornicatrix" or "Incontinent." See 1. 29 and note.

PHYSICIAN.
    I will defame thee ever.
JANE.   Spare me not.
PHYSICIAN.
    I will produce thy bastard, bring thee to public
    Penance.
JANE.   No matter, I care not;
    I shall then have a clean sheet; I'll wear twenty
    Rather than one defil'd with thee.
PHYSICIAN.   Look for revenge!   30
JANE.
    Pursue it fully, then. —[*Aside.*] Out of his hate
    I shall escape, I hope, a loathed fate.   *Exit* Jane.
PHYSICIAN.
    Am I rejected, all my baits nibbled off,
    And not the fish caught? I'll trouble the whole stream
    And choke it in the mud! Since hooks not take,   35
    I'll throw in nets that shall or kill or break.

                Enter Trimtram *with rosemary.*

    This is the bridegroom's man. —Hark, sir, a word.
TRIMTRAM.
    'Tis a busy day, sir, nor I need no physic;
    You see I scour about my business.
PHYSICIAN.
    Pray you, a word, sir. Your master is to be married   40
    today?

27–28. I . . . Penance] *this edn.;*   32. escape] *Dyce;* pursue *Q1; line*
in Q1-2 divided bastard/ penance.   *omitted in Q2.*

---

    29. *wear twenty*] A person convicted of premarital incontinence
might be required to walk barefoot in the procession before Mass on
three Sundays, while wearing a sheet and carrying a candle, and
sometimes to stand in the same costume in the square on market day.
In other cases a public acknowledgement of sin at the time of solem-
nizing the marriage in church might suffice (W. H. Hale, *A Series
of Precedents and Proceedings . . . of the Discipline of the Church of
England* [London, 1847], pp. 10, 153–54, 188).
    35. *it*] the fish—Jane.
    36.1. *rosemary*] symbolic of new life; worn at both weddings and
funerals.

TRIMTRAM.

Else all this rosemary's lost.

PHYSICIAN.

I would speak with your master, sir.

TRIMTRAM.

My master, sir, is to be married this morning and cannot be within while soon at night.   45

PHYSICIAN.

If you will do your master the best service
That e'er you did him, if he shall not curse
Your negligence hereafter slacking it,
If he shall bless me for the dearest friend
That ever his acquaintance met withal,   50
Let me speak with him ere he go to church.

TRIMTRAM.

A right physician! You would have none go to the church
nor churchyard till you send them thither. Well, if death
do not spare you yourselves, he deals hardly with you;
for you are better benefactors and send more to him than   55
all diseases besides.

CHOUGH (*within*).

What, Trimtram, Trimtram!

TRIMTRAM.

I come, sir! Hark you, you may hear him; he's upon the
spur and would fain mount the saddle of matrimony;
but if I can, I'll persuade him to come to you.   60

Exit Trimtram.

PHYSICIAN.

Pray you, do, sir. —I'll teach all peevish niceness
To beware the strong advantage of revenge.

Enter Chough.

CHOUGH.

Who's that would speak with me?

75–76.] *Dyce; prose in Q1–2.*

---

45. *while soon*] until towards. Trim's remark is hard to interpret.
48. *hereafter slacking it*] hereafter saying that you slacked your
best chance of service.
61. *peevish niceness*] perverse coyness.

PHYSICIAN.   None but a friend, sir.

I would speak with you.

CHOUGH.

Why, sir, and I dare speak with any man under the uni-   65
verse. Can you roar, sir?

PHYSICIAN.

No, in faith, sir.

I come to tell you mildly for your good,

If you please to hear me—you are upon marriage?

CHOUGH.

No, sir, I am towards it, but not upon it yet.   70

PHYSICIAN.

Do you know what you do?

CHOUGH.

Yes, sir, I have practic'd what to do before now; I would
be asham'd to be married else. I have seen a bronstrops
in my time, and a hippocrene, and a tweak too.

PHYSICIAN.

Take fair heed, sir; the wife that you would marry   75
Is not fit for you.

CHOUGH.

Why, sir, have you tried her?

PHYSICIAN.

Not I, believe it, sir; but believe withal,

She has been tried.

CHOUGH.

Why, sir, is she a fructifer? Or a fucus?   80

PHYSICIAN.

All that I speak, sir, is in love to you;

Your bride, that may be, has not that portion

That a bride should have.

CHOUGH.

Why, sir, she has a thousand and a better penny!

82–83.] *Dyce; prose in Q1–2.*

---

74. *tweak*] harlot. The first citation in *OED* is to this play.

84. *a better penny*] and even more. Proverbial (Tilley, P 189). "A
thousand gold pieces and more" (Sampson).

PHYSICIAN.

    I do not speak of rubbish, dross, and ore,   85
    But the refined metal *honor*, sir.

CHOUGH.

    What she wants in honor shall be made up in worship,
    sir; money will purchase both.

PHYSICIAN.

    To be plain with you, she's naught.

CHOUGH.

    If thou canst not roar, th'art a dead man! My bride 90
    naught?   *Draws his sword.*

PHYSICIAN.

    Sir, I do not fear you that way. What I speak, [*Draws sword.*]
    My life shall maintain; I say she's naught.

CHOUGH.

    Dost thou not fear me?

PHYSICIAN.

    Indeed I do not, sir.   95

CHOUGH.

    I'll never draw upon thee while I live for that trick. Put
    up and speak freely.

PHYSICIAN.

    Your intended bride is a whore; that's freely, sir.

CHOUGH.

    Yes, faith, a whore's free enough, and she hath a con-
    science. Is she a whore? 'Foot, I warrant she has the pox, 100
    then?

PHYSICIAN.

    Worse, the plague. 'Tis more incurable.

CHOUGH.

    A plaguy whore? A pox on her! I'll none of her.

PHYSICIAN.

    Mine accusation shall have firm evidence.
    I will produce an unavoided witness,   105
    A bastard of her bearing.

91. S.D.] *Dyce; after l. 89 in Q1–2.*   96. thee] *Q2;* the *Q1.*

---

    89. *naught*] immoral (*OED* citing the present passage).
    105. *unavoided*] unavoidable, i.e., unimpeachable (Sampson).

CHOUGH.

> A bastard? 'Snails, there's great suspicion she's a whore,
> then. I'll wrestle a fall with her father for putting this
> trick upon me, as I am a gentleman.

PHYSICIAN.

> Good sir, mistake me not; I do not speak   110
> To break the contract of united hearts;
> I will not pull that curse upon my head,
> To separate the husband and the wife.
> But this, in love, I thought fit to reveal,
> As the due office betwixt man and man,   115
> That you might not be ignorant of your ills.
> Consider now of my premonishment
> As yourself shall please.

CHOUGH.

> I'll burn all the rosemary to sweeten the house, for, in
> my conscience, 'tis infected. Has she drunk bastard? If   120
> she would piss me wine vinegar now nine times a day,
> I'd never have her; and I thank you too.

Enter Trimtram.

TRIMTRAM.

> Come, will you come away, sir? They have all rosemary
> and stay for you to lead the way.

CHOUGH.

> I'll not be married today, Trimtram. Hast e'er an almanac 125
> about thee? This is the nineteenth of August; look what
> day of the month 'tis.   [Trimtram] *looks in an almanac.*

TRIMTRAM.

> 'Tis tenty-nine, indeed, sir.

CHOUGH.

> What's the word? What says Bretnor?

---

120. *bastard*] a sweet Spanish wine.

128. *tenty-nine*] glossed by Dyce and Sampson as meaning nineteen,
but without citation of any authority. The form is not found in
OED or dialect dictionaries; I suspect that *tenty-nine* is a printer's
error for "twenty-nine."

TRIMTRAM.

The word is, sir, "There's a hole in her coat." 130

CHOUGH.

I thought so; the physician agrees with him. I'll not marry today.

TRIMTRAM.

I pray you, sir, there will be charges for new rosemary else; this will be wither'd by tomorrow.

CHOUGH.

Make a bonfire on't to sweeten Rosemary Lane. Prithee, 135 Trim, entreat my father-in-law that might have been to come and speak with me.

TRIMTRAM.

The bride cries already and looks tother way; and you be so backward, too, we shall have a fine arseward wedding on't. *Exit* Trimtram. 140

CHOUGH.

You'll stand to your words, sir?

PHYSICIAN.

I'll not fly the house, sir; when you have need, Call me to evidence. *Exit* Physician.

CHOUGH.

If you'll prove she has borne a bastard, I'll stand to't she's a whore. 145

142–43.] *this edn.; prose in Q1–2; in Dyce lines end* sir/ evidence.

---

129. *word . . . Bretnor*] Like other astrologers Thomas Bretnor classified each day as good or bad and supplied for each an appropriate motto. For 19 August 1617, a good day, he has "Winke at small faults" (see IV.i.149); but "A hole in her coat" does not occur anywhere in the almanacs for 1615, 1616, and 1617. (See also the note to III.ii.32–33.)

130. *There's . . . coat*] proverbial for a person who, having been guilty of sexual sin, is open to gossip, criticism, or charges in an ecclesiastical court. Cf. Robert Greene, *A Quip for an Upstart Courtier*, 1592: "If any man hath got his maid with child or plaies the good felow with his neighbours wife, if [the summoner] finde a hole in any mans coate that is of wealth, then he hath his peremptory scitation . . ." (sig. D2r).

135. *Rosemary Lane*] a short distance outside Aldgate, easternmost entry to the City; the Lane was a place of old clothes shops and a haunt of whores and thieves (Sugden).

Enter Russell *and* Trimtram.

RUSSELL.

Why, how now, son, what causeth these delays?
All stay for your leading.

CHOUGH.

Came I from the Mount to be confronted?

RUSSELL.

How's that, sir?

CHOUGH.

Canst thou roar, old man? 150

RUSSELL.

Roar? How mean you, sir?

CHOUGH.

Why, then, I'll tell thee plainly thy daughter is a bronstrops.

RUSSELL.

A bronsterop? What's that, sir?

TRIMTRAM.

Sir, if she be so, she is a hippocrene. 155

CHOUGH.

Nay, worse, she is a fructifer.

TRIMTRAM.

Nay, then, she is a fucus, a minotaur, and a tweak.

RUSSELL.

Pray you, speak to my understanding, sir.

CHOUGH.

If thou wilt have it in plain terms, she is a callicut and
a panagron. 160

TRIMTRAM.

Nay, then, she is a duplar and a sindicus.

RUSSELL.

Good sir, speak English to me.

CHOUGH.

All this is Cornish to thee. I say thy daughter has drunk
bastard in her time.

152. is] *Q2;* in *Q1.*

---

148. *Mount*] St. Michael's Mount.

RUSSELL.

Bastard? You do not mean to make her a whore?   165

CHOUGH.

Yes, but I do; if she make a fool of me, I'll ne'er make
her my wife till she have her maidenhead again!

RUSSELL.

A whore? I do defy this calumny.

CHOUGH.

Dost thou? I defy thee, then.

TRIMTRAM.

Do you, sir? Then I defy thee, too! Fight with us both 170
at once in this quarrel, if thou darest.

CHOUGH.

I could have had a whore at Plymouth.

TRIMTRAM.

Aye, or at Pe'ryn.

CHOUGH.

Aye, or under the Mount.

TRIMTRAM.

Or as you came, at Evil.   175

CHOUGH.

Or at Hockey Hole in Somersetshire.

TRIMTRAM.

Or at the hanging stones in Wiltshire.

CHOUGH.

Or at Maidenhead in Berkshire; and did I come in by
Maidenhead to go out by Staines? Oh, that man, woman, or child would wrestle with me for a pound of 180
patience!

---

173. *Pe'ryn*] Penryn, on Falmouth Bay, Cornwall.

175. *Evil*] more properly spelled Ivil or Yeovil; in southeastern
Somersetshire.

176. *Hockey Hole*] or Wookey Hole, a cave near Wells, only less
famous than the cave of the Peak, Derbyshire.

177. *hanging stones*] Stonehenge.

178. *Maidenhead*] a town of resort for Londoners, twenty-five miles
west of the City, near the Thames.

179. *Staines*] also a resort on the Thames, seventeen miles west.

RUSSELL.

> Some thief has put in poison at your ears
> To steal the good name of my child from me;
> Or if it be a malice of your own,
> Be sure I will enforce a proof from you.   185

CHOUGH.

> He's a goose and a woodcock that says I will not prove
> any word that I speak.

TRIMTRAM.

> Aye, either goose or woodcock he shall, sir, with any
> man.

CHOUGH.

> Phy-si-ci-an, *mauz avez*, Physician!   190

> [*Enter* Physician.]

RUSSELL.

> Is he the author?

PHYSICIAN.

> Sir, with much sorrow for your sorrow's sake,
> I must deliver this most certain truth:
> Your daughter is an honor-stained bride.
> Indeed, she is the mother to a child   195
> Before the lawful wife unto a husband.

CHOUGH.

> Law, that's worse than I told thee; I said she had borne
> a bastard, and he says she was the mother on't, too.

RUSSELL.

> I'm yet an infidel against all this,
> And will believe the sun is made of brass,   200
> The stars of amber—

CHOUGH.

> And the moon of a Holland cheese.

---

190. *mauz avez*] probably Rowley's rough attempt to spell three
Cornish words which someone pronounced for him: *mos a ves*, "[to]
go outside." (The imperative, which Rowley probably failed to ask
for, is *ke a ves*.) (Edwin Norris, *The Ancient Cornish Drama*, 2 [Ox-
ford, 1858]: 284–85, 292.) Sampson conjectures that *mauz avez* is a
printer's error for Rowley's *man-zaver* (southwestern dialect); but I
see no attempt at this dialect elsewhere in the play.

RUSSELL.
>Rather than this impossibility.
>Oh, here she comes.

>>*Enter* Jane *and* Anne.

>Nay, come, daughter, stand at the bar of shame;   205
>Either now quit thyself, or kill me ever;
>Your marriage day is spoil'd if all be true.

JANE [*aside*].
>A happy misery! —Who's my accuser?

PHYSICIAN.
>I am, that knows it true I speak.

CHOUGH.
>Yes, and I'm his witness.   210

TRIMTRAM.
>And I.

CHOUGH.
>And I again.

TRIMTRAM.
>And I again, too, there's four; that's enough, I hope.

RUSSELL.
>How can you witness, sir, that nothing know
>But what you have receiv'd from his report?   215

CHOUGH.
>Must we not believe our physicians? Pray you, think I
>know as much as every fool does.

TRIMTRAM.
>Let me be Trimtram; I pray you, too, sir.

JANE.
>Sir, if this bad man have laid a blemish
>On my white name, he is a most false one,   220
>Defaming me for the just denial
>Of his foul lust. —Nay, now you shall be known, sir.

ANNE.
>Sir, I'm his sister and do better know him
>Than all of you; give not too much belief
>To his wild words; he's oftentimes mad, sir.   225

203–4.] *Dyce; not divided in Q1–*
2.

PHYSICIAN.

    I thank you, good sister.

ANNE.   Are you not mad to do

    This office? Fie upon your malice!

PHYSICIAN.

    I'll presently produce both nurse and child,

    Whose very eyes shall call her mother before it speaks. [*Exit.*]

CHOUGH.

    Ha, ha, ha, ha! By my troth, I'd spend a shilling on that 230
    condition to hear that; I think in my conscience I shall
    take the Physician in a lie. If the child call her mother
    before it can speak, I'll never wrestle while I live again.

TRIMTRAM.

    It must be a she child if it do, sir, and those speak the
    soonest of any living creatures, they say.   235

CHOUGH.

    Baw, waw! A dog will bark a month sooner; he's a very
    puppy, else.

RUSSELL.

    Come, tell truth twixt ourselves; here's none but friends;
    One spot a father's love will soon wipe off.
    The truth! And thus try my love abundant;   240
    I'll cover it with all the care I have
    And yet, perhaps, make up a marriage day.

JANE.

    Then it's true, sir; I have a child.

RUSSELL.   Hast thou?

    Well, wipe thine eyes; I'm a grandfather then.
    If all bastards were banish'd, the city would be thin   245
    In the thickest term time. Well, now let me alone;
    I'll try my wits for thee. [*Calls.*] Richard, Francis, Andrew!
    None of my knaves within?

Enter his Servant.

226–27.] *this edn.; by Dyce di-*
vided mad/ malice; *in Q1–2*
office/ malice.

240. thus . . . abundant;] *this*

edn.; they . . . abundant, *Q1–2;*
thereby . . . abundant; *Dyce, Bul-*
len, Sampson.

243. have a child] *Q2;* have child
Q1.

SERVANT.

Here's one of 'em, sir. The guests come in apace.

RUSSELL.

Do they, Dick? Let 'em have wine and sugar; we'll be   250
for 'em presently. But hark, Dick.

CHOUGH.

I long to hear this child speak, i'faith, Trim; I would this
foolish Physician would come once.

TRIMTRAM.

If it calls her mother, I hope it shall never call you
father.   255

CHOUGH.

No, and it do, I'll whip it, i'faith, and give thee leave to
whip me.

RUSSELL.

Run on thy best legs, Dick.

SERVANT.

I'll be here in a twinkling, sir.   *Exit* Servant.

Enter Physician *and* Dutch Nurse *with the child.*

PHYSICIAN.

Now, gentlemen, believe your eyes, if not my tongue.   260
[*To* Jane.]   Do not you call this your child?

CHOUGH.

Phew, that's not the point. You promis'd us the child
should call her mother; if it does this month, I'll ne'er
go to the roaring school again.

RUSSELL.

Whose child is this, nurse?   265

NURSE.

Dis gentleman's, so he to me readen.

                            Points to the Physician.

---

266. *readen*] said (German *reden*, not Dutch *raden*). Though Russell
has ample reason to believe that Jane is mother of the child, he surely
cannot believe that the Physician is its father. In performance of the
play Russell's implausible failure at once to suspect Fitzallen of
being the father would not strike the audience's attention because it
is distracted by Russell's cunning maneuvers to make a quick marriage
for Jane.

CHOUGH,

'Snails, she's the Physician's bronstrops, Trim.

TRIMTRAM.

His fucus, his very tweak, i'faith.

CHOUGH.

A glister in his teeth! Let him take her, with a purga-
tion to him.   270

RUSSELL.

'Tis as your sister said; you are stark mad, sir;
This much confirms it. You have defamed
Mine honest daughter; I'll have you punish'd for't,
Besides the civil penance of your sin,
And keeping of your bastard.

PHYSICIAN.   This is fine!   275

All your wit and wealth must not thus carry it.

RUSSELL.

Sir Chough, a word with you.

CHOUGH.

I'll not have her, i'faith, sir. If Trimtram will have her,
and he will, let him.

TRIMTRAM.

Who, I, sir? I scorn it; if you'll have her, I'll have her 280
too. I'll do as you do, and no otherwise.

RUSSELL.,

I do not mean't to either; this only, sir,
That whatsoe'er you've seen, you would be silent;
Hinder not my child of another husband,
Though you forsake her.   285

CHOUGH.

I'll not speak a word, i'faith.

RUSSELL.

As you are a gentleman.

282. mean't] *Dyce;* meant *Q1;*
meane *Q2.*

---

269. *glister*] enema.
274. *civil penance*] punishment in canon law; see the notes to ll.
24 and 29, above.

CHOUGH.

> By these basket hilts, as I am a youth, a gentleman, a
> roarer.

RUSSELL.

> Charm your man, I beseech you, too.   290

CHOUGH.

> I warrant you, sir, he shall do nothing but what I do
> before him.

Enter Servant *with* Fitzallen.

RUSSELL.

> I shall most dearly thank you. —Oh, are you come?
> Welcome, son-in-law! This was beyond your hope;
> We old men have pretty conceits sometimes.   295
> Your wedding day's prepar'd, and this is it.
> How think you of it?

FITZALLEN.   As of the joyfull'st

> That ever welcom'd me; you show yourself now
> A pattern to all kind fathers. —My sweetest Jane!

RUSSELL.

> Your captivity I meant but as sauce   300
> Unto your wedding dinner; now, I'm sure,
> 'Tis far more welcome in this short restraint
> Than had it freely come.

FITZALLEN.   A thousandfold.

JANE.

> I like this well.

CHOUGH [*to* Trimtram].

> I have not the heart to see this gentleman gull'd so. I   305
> will reveal; I make it mine own case; 'tis a foul case.

TRIMTRAM.

> Remember, you have sworn by your hilts.

---

288. *basket hilts*] hilts of wicker work or narrow steel plates, in
basket shape, to protect the swordsman's hand.

290. *Charm*] calm, soothe (*OED*); hence, "silence."

295. *conceits*] ideas.

306. *foul case*] with puns on the senses "ugly body" and "ugly
costume."

CHOUGH.

I'll break my hilts rather than conceal. I have a trick. Do
thou follow me; I will reveal it, and yet not speak it
neither.   310

TRIMTRAM.

'Tis my duty to follow you, sir.

CHOUGH [sings].

Take heed in time, O man, unto thy head!

TRIMTRAM [sings].

All is not gold that glistereth in bed.

RUSSELL.

Why, sir! Why, sir!

CHOUGH [sings].

Look to't, I say; thy bride's a bronsterops!   315

TRIMTRAM [sings].

And knows the thing that men wear in their slops.

FITZALLEN.

How's this, sir?

CHOUGH [sings].

A hippocrene, a tweak, for and a fucus!

TRIMTRAM [sings].

Let not fond love with foretops so rebuke us.

RUSSELL.

Good sir!   320

CHOUGH [sings].

Behold a baby of this maid's begetting!

TRIMTRAM [sings].

A deed of darkness after the sun-setting.

RUSSELL.

Your oath, sir!

CHOUGH [sings].

I swear and sing thy bride has taken physic!

---

312. S.D. *sings*] This way of evading the promise not to speak may
have been borrowed from Thomas Heywood; see *The Rape of Lucrece*
(1608), in *The Dramatic Works,* ed. E. H. Shepheard (London, 1874),
5: 232–33.

316. *slops*] wide, loose breeches.

318. *for and*] and moreover.

319. *foretops*] figuratively, cuckold's horns.

TRIMTRAM [*sings*].

> *This was the doctor cur'd her of that phthisic.* 325

CHOUGH [*sings*].

> *If you'll believe me, I will say no more!*

TRIMTRAM [*sings*].

> *Thy bride's a tweak, as we do say that roar.*

CHOUGH.

Bear witness, gentlemen, I have not spoke a word; my
hilts are whole still.

FITZALLEN.

This is a sweet epithalamium 330
Unto the marriage bed, a musical
Harmonious *Io!* Sir, you've wrong'd me,
And basely wrong'd me! Was this your cunning fetch,
To fetch me out of prison, forever
To marry me unto a strumpet?

RUSSELL. None of those words, good sir. 335
'Tis but a fault, and 'tis a sweet one, too.
Come, sir, your means is short; lengthen your fortunes
With a fair proffer; I'll put a thousand pieces
Into the scale to help her to weigh it up,
Above the first dowry.

FITZALLEN. Ha, you say well. 340
Shame may be bought out at a dear rate.
A thousand pieces added to her dowry—

RUSSELL.

There's five hundred of 'em to make the bargain;
I have worthy guests coming and would not delude 'em.
Say! Speak like a son to me. 345

FITZALLEN.

Your blessing, sir; we are both yours! Witness, gentlemen, these must be made up a thousand pieces, added to
a first thousand for her dowry, to father that child.

---

332. *Io*] Greek and Latin exclamation of joy; hurrah.
338. *pieces*] gold pieces, each worth twenty-two shillings; the sum,
then, is £1,100.

PHYSICIAN.

Oh, is it out now?

CHOUGH.

For tother thousand I'll do't myself yet.   350

TRIMTRAM.

Or I, if my master will.

FITZALLEN.

The bargain's made, sir; I have the tender
And possession both, and will keep my purchase.

CHOUGH.

Take her e'en to you with all her movables; I'll wear my
bachelor's buttons still.   355

TRIMTRAM.

So will I, i'faith; they are the best flowers in any man's
garden, next to heartsease.

FITZALLEN.

This is as welcome as the other, sir,
And both as the best bliss that e'er on earth.
I shall enjoy, sir; this is mine own child.   360
You could not have found out a fitter father,
Nor is it basely bred as you imagine,
For we were wedded by the hand of heaven
Ere this work was begun.

CHOUGH.

At Pancridge, I'll lay my life on't!   365

TRIMTRAM.

I'll lay my life on't, too, 'twas there.

FITZALLEN.

Somewhere it was, sir.

RUSSELL.   Was't so, i'faith, son?

---

349. *is . . . now*] The Physician perceives that Russell believes the
baby is Jane's; cf. ll. 272–73 above.

353. *possession*] Fitzallen takes Jane's hand.

358. *This*] the baby.

365. *Pancridge*] Saint Pancras Church, a somewhat isolated rural
church about two miles northwest of Saint Paul's Cathedral; it was
believed that hasty and irregular marriages could be performed there
(Sugden).

JANE.

And that I must have reveal'd to you, sir,

Ere I had gone to church with this fair groom;

[*Points to* Chough.]

But thank this gentleman; he prevented me.—   370

I am much bound unto your malice, sir.

PHYSICIAN.

I am asham'd.

JANE.   Shame to amendment then.

RUSSELL.

Now get you together for a couple of cunning ones!

But, son, a word; the latter thousand pieces

Is now more than bargain.

FITZALLEN.   No, by my faith, sir;   375

Here's witness enough on't, 't must serve to pay my fees.

Imprisonment is costly.

CHOUGH.

By my troth, the old man has gull'd himself finely! Well,

sir, I'll bid myself a guest, though not a groom; I'll dine

and dance and roar at the wedding for all this.   380

TRIMTRAM.

So will I, sir, if my master does.

RUSSELL.

Well, sir, you are welcome; but now, no more words on't

Till we be set at dinner, for there will mirth

Be the most useful for digestion.

See, my best guests are coming.   385

Enter Captain Ager, Surgeon, Lady Ager, Colonel's Sister, *the two* Friends of Ager.

CAPTAIN AGER.

Recover'd, say'st thou!

376. on't, 't must . . . fees.] *this edn.*; ont, 'must . . . fees *Q1–2*; on it; it must serve/ . . . fees, *Dyce.*

368. *must have revealed*] in order to avoid bigamy and its penalties (Gibson, 1: 417).

SURGEON.

> May I be excluded quite out of Surgeons' Hall else.
> Marry, I must tell you the wound was fain to be twice
> corroded; 'twas a plain gastrolophe, and a deep one. But
> I closed the lips on't with bandages and surtures, which is 390
> a kind conjunction of the parts separated against the
> course of nature.

CAPTAIN AGER.

> Well, sir, he is well.

SURGEON.

> I fear'd him, I assure you, Captain, before the surture in
> the belly. It grew almost to a convulsion, and there was 395
> like to be a bloody issue from the hollow vessels of the
> kidneys.
>
> > [Captain Ager *gives him money.*]

CAPTAIN AGER.

> There's that to thank thy news and thy art together.

SURGEON.

> And if your worship at any time stand in need of inci-
> sion, if it be your fortune to light into my hands, I'll 400
> give you the best.   *Exit.*

CAPTAIN AGER.

> Uncle, the noble Colonel's recover'd!

RUSSELL.

> Recovered?
> Then honor is not dead in all parts, coz.

---

387. *Surgeon's Hall*] in Monkswell Street, near Cripplegate. The barbers and surgeons were incorporated as a company by Parliament in 1540; membership was necessary for practice (Sugden).

389. *corroded*] eaten, gnawed; said of the effects of disease.

389. *gastrolophe*] a misprint, says Dyce; but more likely the Surgeon's error for "gastroraphe" (or "gastroraphy"), the sewing up of a belly wound. However, the Surgeon seems to mean the wound itself, not the sewing.

390. *surtures*] sutures (correction by *OED*, citing this line).

391. *kind conjunction*] natural union (Sampson).

395. *It*] the complications. "The generall accidents most to be feared that affect the wounded are Hemoragia, dolor . . . convulsions . ." (Woodall, sig. S1r).

Enter Colonel *with his two* Friends.

1 AGER'S FRIEND.

    Behold him yonder, sir.   405

CAPTAIN AGER [*aside*].

    My much unworthiness is now found out;

    Thou'st not a face to fit it.

1 COLONEL'S FRIEND.   Sir, yonder's Captain Ager.

COLONEL.

    Oh, lieutenant, the wrong I have done his fame

    Puts me to silence! Shame so confounds me

    That I dare not see him.   410

CAPTAIN AGER.

    I never knew how poor my deserts were

    Till he appear'd; no way to give requital.

    Here, shame me lastingly; do't with his own;

               [*Gives Colonel's will to* 1 Ager's Friend.]

    Return this to him. Tell him I have riches

    In that abundance in his sister's love;   415

    These come but to oppress me and confound

    All my deservings everlastingly.

    I never shall requite my wealth in her, say.

    How soon from virtue and an honor'd spirit

    May man receive what he may never merit!   420

COLONEL.

    This comes most happily to express me better;

    For since this will was made, there fell to me

    The manor of Fitzdale; give him that, too.

       [*Returns will, with codicil, to* 1 Captain Ager's Friend.]

    He's like to have charge; there's fair hope

    Of my sister's fruitfulness. For me,   425

    I never mean to change my mistress,

    And war is able to maintain her servant.

---

423. *that*] Presumably the document is a codicil to the will, adding the new manor to the original bequest. The Colonel has come in person to deliver the codicil and to make peace with Ager and Russell. *That* could hardly be a deed of feoffment, for mere delivery of the deed would not legally transfer the real estate (Paul S. Clarkson and Clyde T. Warren, *The Law of Property in Shakespeare and the Elizabethan Drama* [Baltimore, 1942], pp. 117–18).

1 CAPTAIN AGER'S FRIEND.

　　Read there! A fair increase, sir, by my faith;
　　He hath sent it back, sir, with new additions.

CAPTAIN AGER.

　　How miserable he makes me! This enforces me　　　　　430
　　To break through all the passages of shame
　　And headlong fall—

COLONEL.　　　　　　　Into my arms, dear worthy!

CAPTAIN AGER.

　　You have a goodness
　　Has put me past my answers; you may speak
　　What you please now; I must be silent ever.　　　　　435

COLONEL.

　　This day has shown me joy's unvalu'd treasure.
　　I would not change this brotherhood with a monarch,
　　Into which blest alliance sacred heaven
　　Has plac'd my kinsman, and given him his ends.
　　Fair be that quarrel makes such happy friends.　　　　440

　　　　　　　　　　　　　　　　　　　　　Exeunt omnes.

FINIS

---

439. *kinsman*] Fitzallen.

Appendix A

The Additions of Issue 2, Quarto 1

The bibliographical aspects of the Additions have been briefly considered in the Introduction. A few remarks on the evidence of their authorship may be made here.

The textual peculiarities of the Additions indicate Rowley's sole authorship, notably the spelling of the third personal pronoun, *'um*, and of the ending of weak preterites and participles, which is always -*'d*. There are sixteen instances of *'um*, but no other spelling of the pronoun, which Middleton always wrote as *e'm*; and there are eight instances of -*'d*, three of -*ed* (Middleton used -*d* and -*de* about equally, but never -*ed*). (My conceptions of Rowley's spelling are based on examination of two letters believed to be holograph, his plays, and one tract. On Middleton's spelling see "The Early Editions of *A Trick to Catch the Old One*," *The Library*, 5th series, 22 (1967), especially pp. 210–11.)

Stylistically, also, this episode befits Rowley, especially in its incessant puns and rank bawdiness, as well as in its frequency of allusion to persons and places in London. To a far less degree these elements are also found, of course, in Middleton's uncollaborated work; but his characteristic irony is entirely absent from this scene. There is no reason to believe that Middleton contributed to these Additions.

As co-author and leading actor of the company producing *A Fair Quarrel*, Rowley must have had control of the manuscript. Hence he was able not only to prepare it for publication and to furnish a dedication, but also to sell the Additions to Trundle immediately after they had been introduced into the acted play. At the foot of the first page of the Additions (after l. 34) occurs a direction in black letter: "Place this at the latter end of the fourth Act." The position of the direction shows that the printer meant it to guide the gatherer of quires in the bindery; but the wording is such as Rowley might have placed at the top of page 1 of his manuscript, without bothering to consult the quarto to get the number of the preceding signature (H3v).

Hem, within.
Enter Captain Albo, *a Bawd, and a* Whore.

BAWD.

Hark of these hard-hearted bloodhounds! These butchers are e'en as merciless as their dogs; they knock down a woman's fame e'en as it walks the streets by 'em.

WHORE.

And the Captain here that should defend us walks by like John of the apple-loft.   5

CAPTAIN ALBO.

What, for interjections, Priss? *Hem, Evax, Vah!* Let the

0.1. *Hem*] the call of the harlot, as well as a hoot of derision by street-folk. See *Lusty Juventus,* in *A Select Collection of Old English Plays,* ed. W. Carew Hazlitt (London, 1874), 2: 83; and *2 Henry IV,* III.ii.222.

0.2. *Captain Albo*] a pimp who has taken the guise of a "Swaggering Ruffian" such as Samuel Rowlands describes in *Look to It, for I'll Stab Ye,* 1604, rpt. in *The Complete Works,* ed. Alexander Grosart, 1 (Glasgow, 1880): 27. William Rowley offers a similar character, Lothario, in *All's Lost by Lust,* 1633, sig. H3v. Both as swaggerer and Irishman, Albo seems to be a lampoon of Captain Arthur Severus O'Toole, called "The Great O'Toole" (l. 96); but John Taylor's burlesque eulogy by that title (1622) does not indicate that the braggart was also a pimp.

0.2. *Bawd . . . Whore*] Q1–2 sensibly keep these generic names in the S.P. because they are easier for readers to associate with the appropriate age and costume than are the proper names *Meg* and *Priss* (l. 12).

1. *butchers*] Albo and his women are walking by St. Nicholas Shambles in Newgate Street, north of St. Paul's.

5. *John . . . loft*] "doubtless apple-squire (pimp)" (Sampson). In the cozening game in which a whore's customer was to be swindled, the bawd, if a man, played the role of an outraged husband and in underworld jargon was called an "apple-squire" (Dekker, *The Belman of London,* 1608, sigs. H2r–H2v).

6. *for interjections*] "Should I fight on account of cat-calls?"

6. *Evax*] Latin, "hurrah," "bravo."

6. *Vah*] Latin, expressive of astonishment, etc.

carnifexes scour their throats. Thou knowest there is a
curse hangs over their bloody heads; this year there shall
be more butchers' pricks burn'd than of all trades besides.

BAWD.

I do wonder how thou camest to be a captain.   10

CAPTAIN ALBO.

As thou camest to be a bawd, Meg, and Priss to be a
whore; everyone by their deserts.

BAWD.

Bawd and whore? Out, you unprofitable rascal! Hast not
thou been at the new play yet, to teach thee better manners? Truly, they say they are the finest players, and   15
good speakers of gentlewomen of our quality; "bawd"
and "whore" is not mention'd amongst 'em, but the
handsomest narrow-mouth'd names they have for us,
that some of them may serve as well for a lady as for
one of our occupation.   20

WHORE.

Prithee, patroness, let's go see a piece of that play. If
we shall have good words for our money, 'tis as much as
we can deserve, i'faith.

BAWD.

I doubt 'tis too late now; but another time, servant.

CAPTAIN ALBO.

Let's go now, sweet face. I am acquainted with one of   25
the pantomimics; the bulchins will use the Irish captain
with respect, and you two shall be box'd amongst the
better sort.

---

7. *carnifexes*] in earlier Latin, "executioners of slaves"; in medieval
Latin, often "butchers." Rowley applies the word to Derrick the
hangman in *A Search for Money*, 1609, Percy Society Reprints, 2 (London, 1840): 15.

9. *pricks*] skewers, with a quibble.

14. *new play*] "unidentified" (Sampson); but I think the reference
is to *A Fair Quarrel*.

26. *bulchins*] i.e., bulkins, bull-calves; used in contempt (*OED*
cites this line) or endearment.

27. *box'd*] seated in a section of the gallery above the stage or in
one of the cheaper galleries around the auditorium.

WHORE.

Sirrah Captain Albo, I doubt you are but white-liver'd. Look that you defend us valiantly; you know your penance else. Patroness, you remember how you us'd him once?   30

BAWD.

Aye, servant, and I shall never forget it till I use him so again. —Do you remember, Captain?

CAPTAIN ALBO.

Mum, Meg; I will not hear on't now.   35

BAWD.

How I and my Amazons stripp'd you as naked as an Indian.

CAPTAIN ALBO.

Why, Meg!

BAWD.

And then how I bound you to the good behavior in the open fields.   40

WHORE.

And then you strew'd oats upon his hoppers.

CAPTAIN ALBO.

Prithee, sweet face!

WHORE.

And then brought your ducks to nibble upon him, you remember?

CAPTAIN ALBO.

Oh, the remembrance tortures me again! No more, good   45 sweet face.

BAWD.

Well, lead on, sir; but hark a little.

Enter Chough *and* Trimtram.

CHOUGH.

Didst thou bargain for the bladders with the butcher, Trim?

---

39. *good behavior*] possibly a reference to a physical object (a hurdle?).

41. *hoppers*] thighs? (Not in *OED*.)

— 114 —

TRIMTRAM.

Aye, sir, I have 'em here; I'll practice to swim too, sir, 50
and then I may roar with the water at London Bridge.
He that roars by land and by water both is the perfect
roarer.

CHOUGH.

Well, I'll venture to swim, too. If my father-in-law gives
me a good dowry with his daughter, I shall hold up my 55
head well enough.

TRIMTRAM.

Peace, sir, here's practice for our roaring; here's a centaur and two hippocrenes.

CHOUGH.

Offer the jostle, Trim.

[Trimtram *jostles* Captain Albo.]

CAPTAIN ALBO.

Ha! What meanest thou by that? 60

TRIMTRAM.

I mean to confront thee, cyclops.

CHOUGH.

I'll tell thee what 'a means. Is this thy sister?

CAPTAIN ALBO.

How then, sir?

CHOUGH.

Why, then I say she is a bronstrops, and this is a fucus.

WHORE.

No, indeed, sir, we are both fucuses. 65

CAPTAIN ALBO.

Art thou military? Art thou a soldier?

CHOUGH.

A soldier? No, I scorn to be so poor; I am a roarer.

CAPTAIN ALBO.

A roarer?

TRIMTRAM.

Aye, sir, two roarers.

57–58. *centaur*] pimp? roarer?
61. *cyclops*] swordsman? bully? In IV.i.87 the term seems to mean
"sword," unless that line should read ". . . *me*, cyclops?" The mis-
applications of classical terms in this scene do not occur elsewhere.

CAPTAIN ALBO.

Know then, my fresh-water friends, that I am a captain. 70

CHOUGH.

What! And have but two to serve under you?

CAPTAIN ALBO.

I am now retiring the field.

TRIMTRAM.

You may see that by his bag and baggage.

CHOUGH.

Deliver up thy panagron to me.

TRIMTRAM.

And give me thy sindicus. 75

CAPTAIN ALBO.

Deliver?

BAWD.

I pray you, Captain, be contented; the gentlemen seem
to give us very good words.

CHOUGH.

Good words? Aye, if you could understand 'em; the
words cost twenty pound. 80

BAWD.

What is your pleasure, gentlemen?

CHOUGH.

I would enucleate my fructifer.

WHORE.

What says he, patroness?

BAWD.

He would enoculate. I understand the gentleman very
pithily. 85

CAPTAIN ALBO.

Speak, are you gentle or plebeian? Can you give arms?

CHOUGH.

Arms? Aye, sir, you shall feel our arms presently.

---

82. *enucleate*] properly, "to extract the kernel from" (*OED*); but
here possibly Chough's blunder (with a quibble) for "inoculate."
82. *fructifer*] harlot. See note to IV.i.107.
86. *Can . . . arms*] "Have you a coat of arms?"

TRIMTRAM.

'Sault you the women; I'll pepper him till he stinks
again. I perceive what countryman he is; let me alone
with him.   90

CAPTAIN ALBO.

Dar'st thou charge a captain?

TRIMTRAM.

Yes, and discharge upon him, too.

[Trimtram *turns his back.*]

CAPTAIN ALBO.

Foh! 'tis poison to my country; the slave has eaten
pippins. Oh, shoot no more! Turn both thy broadsides
rather than thy poop. 'Tis foul play; my country breeds   95
no poison. I yield—the great O'Toole shall yield on these
conditions.

CHOUGH.

I have given one of 'em a fair fall, Trim.

TRIMTRAM.

Then thus far we bring home conquest. Follow me, Captain; the cyclops doth command.   100

CHOUGH.

Follow me, tweaks; the centaur doth command.

BAWD.

Anything, sweet gentlemen. Wilt please you to lead to
the tavern, where we'll make all friends?

TRIMTRAM.

Why, now you come to the conclusion.

CHOUGH.

Stay, Trim. I have heard your tweaks are like your mer- 105
maids; they have sweet voices to entice the passengers.
Let's have a song, and then we'll set 'em at liberty.

TRIMTRAM.

In the commendation of roaring, not else, sir.

CHOUGH.

Aye, in the commendation of roaring.

95–96. *country . . . poison*] Ireland has no venomous creatures. Irish
sensitivity to Trimtram's offense was proverbial; cf. Dekker, 2 *Honest
Whore*, I.i.185.

101. *tweaks*] whores.

BAWD.

    The best we can, gentlemen.   110

BAWD. WHORE [*sing*].

> *Then here thou shalt resign*
> *Both "captain" and "commander";*
> *That name was never thine,*
> *But "apple-squire" and "pander."*
> *And henceforth will we grant,*   115
> *In pillage or in moneys,*
> *In clothing or provant,*
> *Whate'er we get by conies.*
> > *With ahone, ahone, ahone!*
> > *No cheaters nor decoys*   120
> > *Shall have a share, but alone*
> > *The bravest roaring boys.*

> *Whate'er we get by gulls*
> *Of country or of city;*
> *Old flatcaps or young heirs,*   125
> *Or lawyers' clerks so witty;*
> *By sailors newly landed*
> *To put in for fresh waters;*
> *By wand'ring gander-mooners,*
> *Or muffled late night-walkers.*   130
> > *With ahone, ahone, ahone!* (etc).

111. BAWD. WHORE [*sing*].] *Sing Baud. Q1–2.*

131.] *in Q1–2 reduced to* With a, &c. *ending l. 130 (so also at l. 139).*

---

117. *provant*] an allowance of food.

118. *conies*] dupes (literally, rabbits).

119. *ahone*] Irish, *ocón*, "alas," "Oh woe." Since the song is a jeer at Albo, this traditional Irish lament is used for refrain. The cry is often used in stage and ballad dialect.

120. *cheaters*] dicers.

120. *decoys*] swindlers, sharpers.

125. *flatcaps*] London citizens (from the low-crowned caps they generally wore).

129. *gander-mooners*] husbands who are unfaithful during the month after their wives' confinement.

> *Whate'er we get by strangers,*
> *The Scotch, the Dutch, or Irish;*
> *Or to come nearer home,*
> *By masters of the parish;*   135
> *It is concluded thus,*
> *By all and every wench,*
> *To take of all their coins,*
> *And pay 'em back in French.*
>   *With ahone, ahone, ahone!* (etc).   140

CHOUGH.

Melodious minotaur!

TRIMTRAM.

Harmonious hippocrene!

CHOUGH.

Sweet-breasted bronstrops!

TRIMTRAM.

Most tunable tweak!

CHOUGH.

Delicious duplar!   145

TRIMTRAM.

Putrefactious panagron!

CHOUGH.

Calumnious callicut!

TRIMTRAM.

And most singular sindicus!

BAWD.

We shall never be able to deserve these good words at your hands, gentlemen.   150

CAPTAIN ALBO.

Shake golls with the Captain; he shall be thy valiant friend.

CHOUGH.

Not yet, Captain; we must make an end of our roaring first.

TRIMTRAM.

We'll serve 'em as we did the tobacco-man, lay a curse 155

---

139. *in French*] with the "French disease," syphilis.
151. *golls*] hands.

upon 'em; marry, we'll lay it on gently, because they
have used us so kindly, and then we'll shake golls
together.

WHORE.

As gently as you can, sweet gentlemen.

CHOUGH.

For thee, O pander: mayst thou trudge till the damn'd 160
soles of thy boots fleet into dirt, but never rise into air.

TRIMTRAM.

Next, mayst thou fleet so long from place to place, till
thou beest kick'd out of Fleet Street.

CHOUGH.

As thou hast lived by bad flesh, so rotten mutton be thy
bane.   165

TRIMTRAM.

When thou art dead, may twenty whores follow thee, that
thou mayst go a squire to thy grave.

CAPTAIN ALBO.

Enough for me, sweet faces; let me sleep in my grave.

CHOUGH.

For thee, old sindicus: may I see thee ride in a caroch
with two wheels, and drawn with one horse.   170

TRIMTRAM.

Ten beadles running by, instead of footmen.

CHOUGH.

With every one a whip, 'stead of an Irish dart.

TRIMTRAM.

Forty barbers' basins sounding before, instead of trumpets.

---

164. *mutton*] whore.

169. *caroch*] a stately carriage. The carting of a bawd is described
with exaggeration in ll. 171–79. Because sexual offenses were tried
and punished by church courts, parish disciplinary officers escorted
the cart to the workhouse and there applied the whip to the offender
if flogging had been assigned as part of the punishment. The rabble
enlivened the procession by beating on barbers' basins. For a full
description see *Dekker, 2 Honest Whore*, V.ii.367–439.

172. *Irish dart*] Irish footmen employed by English magnates are
said to have carried this weapon; Bryan, in *2 Honest Whore*, III.i.179–
80, is an Irish footman, but it is not clear that he carries a dart.

BAWD.

This will be comely indeed, sweet gentlemen-roarers.

TRIMTRAM.

Thy ruff starch'd yellow with rotten eggs. 175

CHOUGH.

And mayst thou then be drawn from Holborn to Hounslow Heath.

TRIMTRAM.

And then be burnt to Colebrook for destroying of
Maidenhead.

BAWD.

I will study to deserve this kindness at your hands, gen- 180
tlemen.

CHOUGH.

Now for thee, little fucus: mayst thou first serve out thy
time as a tweak, and then become a bronstrops as she is.

TRIMTRAM.

Mayst thou have a reasonable good spring, for thou art
like to have many dangerous foul falls. 185

CHOUGH.

Mayst thou have two ruffs torn in one week.

TRIMTRAM.

May spiders only weave thy cobweb lawn.

---

175. *starch'd yellow*] Mrs. Anne Turner, one of the poisoners of
Sir Thomas Overbury, was executed in November 1615 wearing, it
is said, a cobweb-lawn (see l. 187 below) ruff starched yellow, as was
her custom (Dyce and Sampson).

176. *Holborn*] the main thoroughfare from the west into London
through Newgate. Offenders were flogged up this street, and convicts
were taken westward up Holborn to Tyburn with the noose around
their necks (Sugden).

176–77. *Hounslow Heath*] The heath adjoining the town of Hounslow, eleven miles west of London on the coach road, was known as
the scene of robberies; and captured robbers were executed there
(Sugden).

178. *Colebrook*] a village five miles east of Windsor (Sugden).

179. *Maidenhead*] a town of resort for Londoners, twenty-five miles
west of the City, near the Thames (Sugden).

187. *cobweb lawn*] a very fine, transparent linen.

CHOUGH.

Mayst thou set up in Rogue Lane.

TRIMTRAM.

Live till thou stink'st in Garden Alleys.

CHOUGH.

And die sweetly in Tower Ditch.   190

WHORE.

I thank you for that, good sir roarer.

CHOUGH.

Come, shall we go now, Trim? My father-in-law stays for me all this while.

TRIMTRAM.

Nay, I'll serve 'em as we did the tobacco-man; I'll bury 'em all together and give 'em an epitaph.   195

CHOUGH.

All together, Trim! Why then the epitaph will be accessory to the sin. Alas, he has kept the door all his lifetime; for pity let 'em lie together in their graves.

CAPTAIN ALBO.

E'en as thou wilt, Trim; and I thank you, too, sir.

TRIMTRAM.

He that the reason would know, let him hark,   200
Why these three were buried near Mary'bone Park:
These three were a pandar, a bawd, and a whore,
That suck'd many dry to the bones before.
Will you know how they liv'd? Here't may be read:
The Low Countries did ever find 'em bread;   205

201. *three*] Dyce; *two* Q1-2.

---

188. *Rogue Lane*] otherwise Shire Lane, a very disreputable suburban street west of the City near the Temple (Sugden).

189. *Garden Alleys*] possibly the gardens around the Temple, where harlots were said to seek customers (Sugden).

190. *Tower Ditch*] the ancient moat around the Tower precincts. The ditch around the city walls of London acted as a sewer and sometimes overflowed into Tower Ditch (Sugden).

197. *sin*] of their lying together. But then for pity Chough decides to allow it.

201. *Mary'bone*] Marylebone, a country village over two miles west of London, near Tyburn (Sugden).

They liv'd by Flushing, by Sluis, and the Groyne,
Sickened in France, and died under the Line.
Three letters at last commended 'em hither,
But the hangman broke one in putting together.
"P" was the first, who cries out for a pardon;   210
"O" craves his book, yet could not read such a hard one;
An "X" was the last, which in conjunction
Was broke by Brandon; and here's the conclusion:
By three trees, three letters; these three—pandar, bawd,
     whore—
Now stink below ground, stunk long above before.   215

CHOUGH.

So, now we have done with you; remember roaring boys.

TRIMTRAM.

Farewell, centaur.

CHOUGH.

Farewell, bronstrops.

TRIMTRAM.

Farewell, fucus.   *Exeunt* Chough *and* Trimtram.

CAPTAIN ALBO.

Well, Meg, I will learn to roar, and still maintain the   220
name of captain over these lanceprisados.

BAWD.

If thou dost not, mayst thou be buried under the roaring curse.   *Exeunt.*

---

206. *Flushing*] a fortified Dutch port on the Scheldt, for almost
twenty years held by the English (Sugden).

206. *Sluis*] a port also on the Scheldt, ten miles east of Bruges
(Sugden).

206. *the Groyne*] Groyning, or Groningen, in Friesland, ninety-five
miles northeast of Amsterdam. These names were familiar to Eng-
lishmen because of England's participation in the wars in the Low
Countries against Spain.

207. *in France*] i.e., of the pox.

207. *the Line*] the equator.

209–14. *hangman . . . letters*] These lines are obscure. Pandering
and whoredom were not felonies; hence no need for the function of
Gregory Brandon, the London hangman, nor for a plea of benefit
of clergy, l. 211. Probably there is a pun on "axe" in l. 212.

221. *lanceprisados*] lance-corporals; the lowest grade of noncom-
missioned officer.

Appendix B

The Roaring School

The idea of a roaring school as a source of hilarity and of satiric comment on the Colonel's conception of honor was perhaps suggested to Rowley by Jonson's *The Alchemist*, III.iv.15–41 (1610); Rowley's use of language in developing the device probably derives from Thomas Bretnor, maker of almanacs, and from John Marston, satirist.

Schools for the teaching of languages, dancing, and fencing were advertised by means of notices affixed to the pillars of St. Paul's Cathedral; and their style is echoed in the "exemplary" of the Roaring School (see *Every Man Out of His Humor*, III.iii.47–65, and *A Fair Quarrel*, IV.i.32–37). But Rowley noted in Bretnor's almanacs for 1615, 1616, and 1617 the astrologer's advertisements (said to have been the first instance of such advertising in almanacs) in this language: "All such as are desirous to be instructed in all or any of the Arts and Sciences vnder mentioned may vpon like terms in short time haue such easie instruction, that by their owne study and proper endeuors they may afterwards easily attaine the full period and scope of their intendments." The subjects for study are arithmetic, geometry, navigation, astronomy, and astrology; and Bretnor offers to teach them in English, Latin, French, or Spanish! (1615, sigs. A1v–A2r). On the title page he describes himself as "professour of the Mathematics & Student in Physicke," and he uses a Latin motto. His pretentiousness evidently amused Rowley; the pedantry in the roarers' mutual vilification seems to have been prompted by Bretnor's expression. Several borrowings from Bretnor are cited in the footnotes.

However, in order fully to translate Bretnor's pomposity into absurd jargon. Rowley probably imitated Marston's bombast, notably that in *Certain Satires*, published with *Pigmalion's Image* (1598):

> Ambitious *Gorgons*, wide-mouth'd *Lamians*,
> Shape-changing *Proteans*, damn'd *Briareans*,
> Is *Minos* dead? is *Radamanth* asleep?
>
> ⋯⋯⋯⋯⋯⋯⋯⋯⋯⋯⋯⋯⋯⋯⋯⋯⋯⋯⋯⋯⋯
>
> What *Myrmidon*, or hard *Dolopian*,
> What savage minded rude *Cyclopian*,
> But such a sweete pathetique *Paphian*
> Would force to laughter? (Signatures E8r, F7r.)

Other English imitators of Roman satire of course published similar extravagance for Rowley to travesty, in order to amuse the more literate members of his audience. His choice of terms seems largely determined by the chance they offer for indecent puns and allusions. In this vein, as in his burlesque of classical allusion and learning in general, Rowley is also following the tradition of Thomas Nashe, writer of tracts, and his imitators, such as Thomas Dekker. Hence the roarers' jargon amused the audience by several overtones of parody.

Appendix C

Chronology

Approximate years are indicated by *, occurrences in doubt by (?).

Political and Literary Events	*Life and Major Works of Middleton and Rowley*
1558 Accession of Queen Elizabeth I. Robert Greene born. Thomas Kyd born.	
1560 George Chapman born.	
1561 Francis Bacon born.	
1564 Shakespeare born. Christopher Marlowe born.	
1572 Thomas Dekker born.* John Donne born. Massacre of St. Bartholomew's Day.	
1573 Ben Jonson born.*	
1574 Thomas Heywood born.*	
1576 The Theatre, the first permanent public theater in London, established by James Burbage. John Marston born.	
1577 The Curtain theater opened.	

Holinshed's *Chronicles of England, Scotland and Ireland.*
Drake begins circumnavigation of the earth; completed 1580.
1578
John Lyly's *Euphues: The Anatomy of Wit.*
1579
John Fletcher born.
Sir Thomas North's translation of Plutarch's *Lives.*
1580

Thomas Middleton born in London, baptized 18 April.

1583
Philip Massinger born.
1584
Francis Beaumont born.*
1585

William Rowley born.*

1586
Death of Sir Philip Sidney.
John Ford born.
Kyd's *THE SPANISH TRAGEDY.*
1587
The Rose theater opened by Henslowe.
Marlowe's *TAMBURLAINE,* Part I.*
Execution of Mary, Queen of Scots.
Drake raids Cadiz.
1588
Defeat of the Spanish Armada.
Marlowe's *TAMBURLAINE,* Part II.*
1589
Greene's *FRIAR BACON AND FRIAR BUNGAY.*
Marlowe's *THE JEW OF MALTA.*
1590
Spenser's *Faerie Queene* (Books I–III) published.

Sidney's *Arcadia* published.
Shakespeare's *HENRY VI*, Parts
I–III,* *TITUS ANDRONICUS.*

1591
Shakespeare's *RICHARD III.*

1592
Marlowe's *DOCTOR FAUSTUS*
and *EDWARD II.*
Shakespeare's *TAMING OF THE
SHREW* and *THE COMEDY OF
ERRORS.*
Death of Greene.

1593
Shakespeare's *LOVE'S LABOR'S
LOST;* *Venus and Adonis* pub-
lished.
Death of Marlowe.
Theaters closed on account of
plague.

1594
Shakespeare's *TWO GENTLE-
MEN OF VERONA;* *The Rape
of Lucrece* published.
Shakespeare's company becomes
Lord Chamberlain's Men.
Death of Kyd.

1595
The Swan theater built.
Sidney's *Defense of Poesy* pub-
lished.
Shakespeare's *ROMEO AND JU-
LIET,* *A MIDSUMMER
NIGHT'S DREAM,* *RICHARD
II.*
Raleigh's first expedition to
Guiana.

1596
Spenser's *Faerie Queene* (Books
IV–VI) published.
Shakespeare's *MERCHANT OF
VENICE,* *KING JOHN.*
James Shirley born.

1597

Bacon's *Essays* (first edition).
Shakespeare's *HENRY IV*, Part I.*

Middleton's first published verse, *The Wisdom of Solomon Paraphrased.*

1598

Demolition of The Theatre.
Shakespeare's *MUCH ADO ABOUT NOTHING,* *HENRY IV*, Part II.*
Jonson's *EVERY MAN IN HIS HUMOR* (first version).
Seven books of Chapman's translation of Homer's *Iliad* published.

Middleton matriculated at Queen's College, Oxford, 7 April.*

1599

The Paul's Boys reopen their theater.
The Globe theater opened.
Shakespeare's *AS YOU LIKE IT,* *HENRY V, JULIUS CAESAR.*
Marston's *ANTONIO AND MELLIDA,* Parts I and II.
Dekker's *THE SHOEMAKERS' HOLIDAY.*
Death of Spenser.

Middleton's *Micro-Cynicon* (poem) published.

1600

Shakespeare's *TWELFTH NIGHT.*
The Fortune theater built by Alleyn.
The Children of the Chapel begin to play at the Blackfriars.

Middleton's *Ghost of Lucrece* (poem) published.
Middleton withdrew from Oxford in the latter half of 1600.

1601

Shakespeare's *HAMLET,* *MERRY WIVES OF WINDSOR.*
Insurrection and execution of the Earl of Essex.
Jonson's *POETASTER.*
BLURT MASTER CONSTABLE (by Dekker?).

1602

Shakespeare's *TROILUS AND CRESSIDA.*

Middleton married to Magdalen (or Mary) Marbeck.*

— 129 —

Middleton's *THE CHESTER TRAGEDY, OR RANDALL EARL OF CHESTER* (lost); Middleton, Dekker, Drayton, Munday, and Webster's *CAESAR'S FALL* (lost) (Admiral's Men).

14 December, Middleton receives 5s. for a prologue and epilogue of *FRIAR BACON AND FRIAR BUNGAY.*

1603

Death of Queen Elizabeth I; accession of James VI of Scotland as James I.

Florio's translation of Montaigne's *Essays* published.

Shakespeare's *ALL'S WELL THAT ENDS WELL.**

Heywood's *A WOMAN KILLED WITH KINDNESS.*

Marston's *THE MALCONTENT.**

Shakespeare's company becomes the King's Men.

Middleton's *THE PHOENIX** (Paul's Boys).

Middleton's *The True Narration of the Entertainment of His Royal Majesty from Edinburgh till London* (?) (pamphlet).

1604

Shakespeare's *MEASURE FOR MEASURE,* OTHELLO.**

Marston's *THE FAWN.**

Chapman's *BUSSY D'AMBOIS.**

Middleton's son Edward born.

Middleton's *The Ant and the Nightingale, or Father Hubbard's Tales; The Black Book* (pamphlets).

Middleton and Dekker's *THE HONEST WHORE*, Part I (Prince Henry's Men).

Middleton's *MICHAELMAS TERM** (Paul's Boys).

1605

Shakespeare's *KING LEAR.**

Marston's *THE DUTCH COURTESAN.**

Bacon's *Advancement of Learning* published.

The Gunpowder Plot.

Middleton's *YOUR FIVE GALLANTS** (originally Paul's Boys?); *A TRICK TO CATCH THE OLD ONE;* A MAD WORLD, MY MASTERS** (both Paul's Boys).

Middleton and Dekker's *THE ROARING GIRL** (Prince Henry's Men).

1606

Shakespeare's *MACBETH.**
Jonson's *VOLPONE.**
The Red Bull theater built.
Death of John Lyly.

Middleton's *THE VIPER AND HER BROOD* (presumably lost); *THE REVENGER'S TRAGEDY** (The King's Men?); *THE PURITAN, OR THE WIDOW OF WATLING STREET** (Paul's Boys).

1607

Shakespeare's *ANTONY AND CLEOPATRA.**
Beaumont's *KNIGHT OF THE BURNING PESTLE.**
Settlement of Jamestown, Virginia.

Rowley, Day, and Wilkins' *THE TRAVELS OF THE THREE ENGLISH BROTHERS.**

1608

Shakespeare's *CORIOLANUS,* TIMON OF ATHENS,* PERICLES.**
Chapman's *CONSPIRACY AND TRAGEDY OF CHARLES, DUKE OF BYRON.**
Richard Burbage leases Blackfriars Theatre for King's company.
John Milton born.

Rowley's *A SHOEMAKER A GENTLEMAN* and (with Heywood) *FORTUNE BY LAND AND SEA** (Queen's Men).

1609

Shakespeare's *CYMBELINE;* Sonnets* published.
Jonson's *EPICOENE.*
Dekker's *Gull's Hornbook* published.

Rowley began his acting career with Prince Charles's Men.
Rowley's *A Search for Money* (pamphlet).
Middleton's *Sir Robert Shirley's Entertainment in Cracovia* (pamphlet).

1610

Jonson's *ALCHEMIST.*
Chapman's *REVENGE OF BUSSY D'AMBOIS.**
Richard Crashaw born.

Rowley's *A NEW WONDER, A WOMAN NEVER VEXED.**

1611

Authorized (King James) Version of the Bible published.

Shakespeare's *THE WINTER'S TALE,** *THE TEMPEST.**

Beaumont and Fletcher's *A KING AND NO KING.*

Tourneur's *ATHEIST'S TRAGEDY.**

Chapman's translation of *Iliad* completed.

Middleton's *A CHASTE MAID IN CHEAPSIDE** (Princess Elizabeth's Men); *THE SECOND MAIDEN'S TRAGEDY(?).**

Middleton and Rowley's *WIT AT SEVERAL WEAPONS(?).**

1612

Webster's *THE WHITE DEVIL.**

Rowley's *HYMEN'S HOLIDAY, OR CUPID'S VAGARIES* (lost).

Middleton's *NO WIT, NO HELP LIKE A WOMAN'S* (Princess Elizabeth's Men[?]).

1613

The Globe theater burned.

Shakespeare's *HENRY VIII* (with Fletcher).

Webster's *THE DUCHESS OF MALFI.**

Sir Thomas Overbury murdered.

Rowley's *A KNAVE IN PRINT* (lost) and *THE FOOL WITHOUT BOOK* (lost).

Middleton began his career of writing for civic and official ceremonies with *THE NEW RIVER ENTERTAINMENT* and *THE TRIUMPHS OF TRUTH,* the latter for the induction of Sir Thomas Middleton as Lord Mayor.

1614

The Globe theater rebuilt.

The Hope Theatre built.

Jonson's *BARTHOLOMEW FAIR.*

Middleton's *THE MASQUE OF CUPID* (lost).

Middleton and Rowley's *THE OLD LAW** (Queen Henrietta's Men?) (revised by Massinger).

1615

Middleton's *THE WITCH** and *MORE DISSEMBLERS BESIDES WOMEN** (both King's Men).

1616

Publication of Folio edition of Jonson's *Works.*

Middleton's *THE MAYOR OF QUINBOROUGH, OR HENGIST*

Chapman's *Whole Works of Homer*.
Death of Shakespeare.
Death of Beaumont.

KING OF KENT; *THE WID-OW;* *THE NICE VALOR* (with Fletcher?) (all King's Men). Middleton's *CIVITATIS AMOR* for the reception of Charles on his creation as Prince of Wales. Middleton and Rowley's *A FAIR QUARREL* (Prince Charles's Men).

1617

Middleton's *THE TRIUMPHS OF HONOR AND INDUSTRY,* for the Company of Grocers on the induction of one of their members as Lord Mayor.

1618
Outbreak of Thirty Years War.
Execution of Raleigh.
1619

Middleton's *The Peacemaker* (pamphlet).

Middleton's *INNER TEMPLE MASQUE, OR MASQUE OF HEROES* (Prince Charles's Men); *THE TRIUMPHS OF LOVE AND ANTIQUITY* (Lord Mayor's show); *On the Death of Richard Burbage* (elegy). Rowley's *ALL'S LOST BY LUST* (Prince Charles's Men). Middleton and Rowley's *THE WORLD TOSSED AT TENNIS** (Prince Charles's Men).

1620
Settlement of Plymouth, Massachusetts.

Middleton appointed City Chronologer for London, September 6. Middleton's *The Marriage of the Old and New Testaments*(?) (pamphlet). Rowley's *THE BIRTH OF MERLIN.**

1621
Robert Burton's *Anatomy of Melancholy* published.
Andrew Marvell born.

Middleton's *ANYTHING FOR A QUIET LIFE** (King's Men); *WOMEN BEWARE WOMEN* (King's Men).

Middleton and Munday's (?) *THE SUN IN ARIES,* for the Drapers' Company at the induction of the Lord Mayor; and nine *HONORABLE ENTERTAINMENTS* (for civic occasions).

Rowley, Ford, and Dekker's *THE WITCH OF EDMONTON* (Prince Charles's Men).

1622
Henry Vaughan born.

Middleton and Rowley's *THE CHANGELING* (Princess Elizabeth's Men).

Rowley's *A MATCH AT MIDNIGHT* (Children of the Revels).

Middleton's *AN INVENTION FOR THE LORD MAYOR* (for the Lord Mayor's feast); and *THE TRIUMPHS OF HONOR AND VIRTUE,* for the Grocers' Company at the induction of the Lord Mayor.

1623
Publication of Folio edition of Shakespeare's *COMEDIES, HISTORIES, AND TRAGEDIES.*

Charles and Buckingham visit Spain to negotiate the Prince's marriage to the Infanta.

Rowley joins the King's Men as an actor.

Middleton and Rowley's *THE SPANISH GYPSY* (Princess Elizabeth's Men).

Middleton's *THE TRIUMPHS OF INTEGRITY,* for the Drapers' Company at the induction of the Lord Mayor.

Rowley and Fletcher's *THE MAID IN THE MILL* (King's Men).

1624

Middleton's *A GAME AT CHESS* (King's Men).

Rowley, Ford, Dekker, and Webster's *KEEP THE WIDOW WAKING* (lost).

1625

Death of King James I; accession of Charles I.
Death of Fletcher.

Rowley and Webster's *A CURE FOR A CUCKOLD*.

1626

Death of Tourneur.
Death of Bacon.

Rowley buried at Clerkenwell.
Middleton's *THE TRIUMPHS OF HEALTH AND PROSPERITY*, for the Drapers' Company at the induction of the Lord Mayor.

1627

Middleton buried at Newington Butts, July 4.

1628

Ford's *THE LOVER'S MELANCHOLY*.
Petition of Right.
Buckingham assassinated.

1631

Shirley's *THE TRAITOR*.
Death of Donne.
John Dryden born.

1632

Massinger's *THE CITY MADAM*.*
Death of Dekker.

1633

Donne's *Poems* published.
Death of George Herbert.

1634

Death of Chapman, Marston, Webster.*
Publication of *THE TWO NOBLE KINSMEN*, with title-page attribution to Shakespeare and Fletcher.
Milton's *Comus*.

1635

Sir Thomas Browne's *Religio Medici*.

1637
Death of Jonson.

1639
First Bishops' War.
Death of Carew.*

1640
Short Parliament.
Long Parliament impeaches Laud.
Death of Massinger, Burton.

1641
Irish rebel.
Death of Heywood.

1642
Charles I leaves London; Civil War breaks out.
Shirley's *COURT SECRET*.
All theaters closed by Act of Parliament.

1643
Parliament swears to the Solemn League and Covenant.

1645
Ordinance for New Model Army enacted.

1646
End of First Civil War.

1647
Army occupies London.
Charles I forms alliance with Scots.
Publication of Folio edition of Beaumont and Fletcher's *COMEDIES AND TRAGEDIES*.

1648
Second Civil War.

1649
Execution of Charles I.

1650
Jeremy Collier born.

1651
Hobbes' *Leviathan* published.

1652

First Dutch War begins (ended 1654).

Thomas Otway born.

1653

Nathaniel Lee born.*

1656

D'Avenant's *THE SIEGE OF RHODES* performed at Rutland House.

1657

John Dennis born.

1658

Death of Oliver Cromwell.

D'Avenant's *THE CRUELTY OF THE SPANIARDS IN PERU* performed at the Cockpit.

1660

Restoration of Charles II.

Theatrical patents granted to Thomas Killigrew and Sir William D'Avenant, authorizing them to form, respectively, the King's and the Duke of York's Companies.

1661

Cowley's *THE CUTTER OF COLEMAN STREET*.

D'Avenant's *THE SIEGE OF RHODES* (expanded to two parts).

1662

Charter granted to the Royal Society.

1663

Dryden's *THE WILD GALLANT*.

Tuke's *THE ADVENTURES OF FIVE HOURS*.

1664

Sir John Vanbrugh born.

Dryden's *THE RIVAL LADIES*.

Dryden and Howard's *THE IN-DIAN QUEEN*.

Etherege's *THE COMICAL RE-VENGE*.

1665

Second Dutch War begins (ended 1667).

Great Plague.

Dryden's *THE INDIAN EM-PEROR*.

Orrery's *MUSTAPHA*.

1666

Fire of London.

Death of James Shirley.